THE CALL OF THE HARVEST

THE CALL
OF THE HARVEST

Charles L. McKay

13

13
Convention Press

NASHVILLE   TENNESSEE

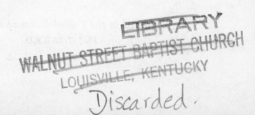

Printed in the United States of America
15. JUL 56 R.R.D.

THIS LITTLE VOLUME IS AFFECTIONATELY
DEDICATED TO MY TWO DAUGHTERS,
RUTH AND JUNE

About the Author

Dr. CHARLES L. McKAY, secretary of enlargement and enlistment for evangelism in the Sunday School Department of the Sunday School Board of the Southern Baptist Convention, is a native Mississippian.

He received his B.A. degree from Mississippi College, and the Th.M. and Th.D. degrees from the New Orleans Baptist Theological Seminary.

Churches that he served, however hard at work at home, never lost sight of the needs of "regions beyond."

Dr. McKay is in constant demand across the nation as evangelist, Bible teacher, assembly speaker, and conference leader.

He is the author of *The Hand of God in Human Experience* and also many tracts on enlargement and evangelism.

The Sunday School Training Course

THE Sunday School Training Course prepared by the Sunday School Department of the Baptist Sunday School Board is one of the major means of promoting Sunday school work. Its influence is limited only by its use.

The six sections of the course include studies in Bible, doctrines, evangelism, Sunday school leadership and administration, teaching, age-group studies, and special studies. The range of the course is broad, for the field of Sunday school work is broad and requires comprehensive and specific training. Sixteen books are required for the completion of each diploma.

The study of the training course is not to be limited to the present Sunday school workers. Most churches need twice as many workers as are now enlisted. This need can be supplied by training additional workers now. Members of the Young People's and Adult classes and older Intermediates should be led to study these books, for thereby will their service be assured. Parents will find help as they study what the Sunday school is trying to do.

Special Note to Instructors

During your teaching of this book will you check with the Sunday school superintendent and see if an accurate record of training for the workers is kept. If not, please urge him to set up such a file with an associate superintendent of training in charge. File cards for this purpose may be ordered at nominal cost from your nearest Baptist Book Store.

A. V. WASHBURN
Secretary, Teaching and Training
Sunday School Department
Baptist Sunday School Board

Contents

Contents

Introduction

THIS BOOK comes out of the successful experiences of a man. It shows how a church can have perennial and maximum results in winning people to Christ.

Dr. Charles L. McKay was pastor in Mobile, Alabama, for several years; also pastor in Pascagoula, Mississippi, for a period of years. This pastor and people working together in these churches demonstrated that the plans and methods presented in this book are right and, when used, they are fruitful.

Dr. McKay not only believes that the Bible is man's sufficient guide in faith and practice, but he puts his belief into practice in his own life and also in the life and work in the churches.

He believes in people. He found by experience that people will serve happily and successfully in the work of a church when properly approached. He discovered that Christian men and women will prepare themselves to work acceptably in a church when opportunities are provided.

Dr. McKay learned out of experience that the Sunday school can be used to provide places of service for the church members. He also learned out of experience that when the church members are organized and trained for work, the Sunday school can be used to get the work of a church accomplished more completely than any other known way. In the churches where Dr. McKay served as pastor, the results of the work in evangelism, enlistment of people in service, giving, reaching the people for all the activities in a church, Christian homes, and Christian living testify to the rightness of the teachings in this book.

I count it a happy privilege to write this word of introduction. I can enthusiastically commend this book to pastors, educational directors, Sunday school superintendents, and all other Sunday school workers. Because of the content of the book, it is a conviction of my heart that it would be a most profitable experience for every pastor in our great Convention to study this book with the Sunday school workers, and begin and continue to put into fuller practice the basic plans and practical methods presented.

J. N. BARNETTE

1

The Necessity for Evangelism

"Wherefore, as by one man sin entered into the world, and death by sin; and so death passed upon all men, for that all have sinned" (Rom. 5:12).

ONLY THE BIBLE reveals what actually happened to bring about the absolute necessity for evangelism. "Sin entered into the world." That is what has caused the many terrible and drastic changes in the lives of all men, many of which we hesitate to discuss or even mention. Man's condition since the fall necessitates a plan and program whereby estranged, condemned sinners may be reconciled to a righteous God. Bible evangelism is the answer.

The strife among nations that breeds wars and rumors of wars did not create the need for a program of evangelism. The need did not come because capital and labor could not always be in agreement. Nor did it come because of conflicting ideas about racial relationships. It was not due to a slip or stumble of man by mistake. The need for evangelism is due to the fall of man. As the Bible states, "There is none righteous, no, not one: . . . For all have sinned, and come short of the glory of God" (Rom. 3:10, 23).

I. SIN MAKES EVANGELISM NECESSARY

Man is a sinner. If he has accepted Jesus Christ as his personal Saviour, he is a sinner saved by grace; if he has not accepted Christ as his Saviour, he is a lost sinner. All men are sinners; therefore evangelism is essential. New Testament churches are necessary for New Testament evangelism.

1

Sin has brought about the need for church-centered evangelism.

1. The Fact of Sin Creates the Need for Evangelism

Sin is a fact, and only a fool will deny it (Prov. 14:9). This is the only basic need for the gospel of Christ. "Christ died for our sins according to the scriptures" (1 Cor. 15:3). If Paul had not realized the sin principle in his own life, he never would have said, "Christ Jesus came into the world to save sinners; of whom I am chief" (1 Tim. 1:15).

(1) *Christ died for sin.*—If sin is not a fact, then Jesus made the biggest blunder of history when he died on the cross. If men are not lost in sin, then Christ died in vain. Look at it from any angle you will—sin is a reality. Do not try to hide it. It cannot be overlooked. It must be faced rightly, and the only one who can meet sin and deal adequately with it is Jesus Christ. He is the match for sin. He knows how to deal with this great malady.

(2) *Sin abounds.*—One cannot evade the issue of sin. Pass a hospital and be reminded of its reality. Look at the graveyard and remember where death originated. Read about the crime wave and remember that the devil is the ringleader of the great army of criminals in America and elsewhere.

See that bloody war that took its toll and ask, "Why bloody war?" Examine every broken home where divorce has invaded and done its dirty work and remember that God hates divorce (Mal. 2:16). Visit the jails, where thieves, murderers, drunkards, and lawless criminals are, and remember that sin is a reproach to any people. The evidences of sin are so many that we concur with the teachings of the Scriptures that the whole world is guilty before God, for all have sinned.

2. The Nature of Sin Makes Evangelism Necessary

People do not need to be told that they are sinners; they know it. "Let no man say when he is tempted, I am tempted of God: for God cannot be tempted with evil, neither tempteth he any man: but every man is tempted, when he is drawn away of his own lust, and enticed. Then when lust hath conceived, it bringeth forth sin: and sin, when it is finished, bringeth forth death" (James 1:13-15).

Sin is missing the mark of holiness. It is failure to measure up to God's standard of excellence. It is coming short of perfection. Sin is rebellion against God's will. "All unrighteousness is sin" (1 John 5:17).

The voluntary transgression of known law is sin. The Bible refers to the origin and nature of sin as the free act of the first parents by which they turned away from God. They brought themselves under the penalty of the law. Seeking to become wise as gods, they became slaves to the devil. They changed masters of their own free will and accord. The human blood stream was corrupted at the fountain, and every child born of man since the fall has been a problem child—morally and spiritually—because of sin.

"To him that knoweth to do good, and doeth it not, to him it is sin" (James 4:17). "For whatsoever is not of faith is sin" (Rom. 14:23). Jesus said that anger in one's heart could be murder—just as much as the act itself. A state or disposition can as easily be sin as is the overt act. Impure desire in one's heart is adultery. There are sins of omission and sins of commission.

3. *The Origin of Sin Makes Evangelism Necessary*

In Genesis 3:1 we find the source of the temptation is the tempter himself. "Now the serpent was more subtil than any beast of the field which the Lord God had made. And he said unto the woman, Yea, hath God said, Ye shall not eat of every tree of the garden?" Evidently, this serpent was the most subtle of all God's creation. The Genesis account reveals him to us as cunning, tricky, deceitful, yet beautiful. He had all the qualities that go to make up subtleness. But his name was legion.

(1) *The serpent.*—The tempter is called the serpent. Satan came to the first woman in the form of the serpent. We should not think of the serpent at the time of this temptation as a beast that crawled in the dirt, as we find him doing after

the curse of God was placed upon him. The prophet Isaiah spoke of "fiery flying serpents." It is possible that the deceiver, called "the serpent," was once a thing of beauty having wings with which to fly.

(2) *The devil.*—His name is "the devil." When Jesus spoke of our tempter, he said, "Ye are of your father the devil, and the lusts of your father ye will do. He was a murderer from the beginning" (John 8:44). Is it any wonder that Satan committed murder in the garden of Eden when he caused to die the first man and woman? Yes, they died, both physically and spiritually. Of course, it took time for sin to run its course in bringing about physical death to our parents, but spiritual death took place immediately. They were cast off from the presence of God.

(3) *A liar.*—"A liar" our tempter is called. Jesus called him "a liar, and the father of it" (John 8:44). The first record of a lie in the Bible is recorded in Genesis 3. He lied to the woman; he caused death to come to the first pair; he murdered them. He lied and became the originator, or the father, of lies.

(4) *Angel of light.*—Paul said, "For such are false apostles, deceitful workers, transforming themselves into the apostles of Christ. And no marvel; for Satan himself is transformed into an angel of light" (2 Cor. 11:13–14). The serpent tried to convince Eve that he was wiser than God. He made it appear to her that God was a deceiver and that he was withholding from her that which she should have. Thus, the serpent led the first woman to doubt the veracity of God.

(5) *Prince of the power of the air.*—"Prince of the power of the air" is another name given to the serpent. Paul said, "Wherein in time past ye walked according to the course of this world, according to the prince of the power of the air, the spirit that now worketh in the children of disobedience" (Eph. 2:2).

(6) *Adversary.*—Simon Peter adds yet another name. He said, "Be sober, be vigilant; because your adversary the devil, as a roaring lion, walketh about, seeking whom he may devour" (1 Peter 5:8).

(7) *Dragon.*—The book of Revelation reveals yet another name for our tempter. "And the great dragon was cast out, that old serpent, called the Devil, and Satan, which deceiveth the whole world" (Rev. 12:9).

Man's tempter is not just another man; he is superhuman with superpower. Therefore we must have some unseen strength to help us conquer him. This power God offers us through his Holy Spirit. God's redemption is available for all men. God's method for making redemption from sin known to all men is evangelism.

4. The Tragedy of Sin Makes Evangelism Necessary

Adam's sin ruined not only him, but it extended the ruin to all his posterity.

(1) *All have sinned.*—When Adam transgressed and by choice disobeyed God, his new master, the devil, ejected something into man's system far worse than poison. The sin principle entered the blood stream at the fountain, and we are all by nature children of wrath (Eph. 2:3). That is exactly what Paul means when he says, "Wherefore, as by one man sin entered into the world, and death by sin; and so death passed upon all men, for that all have sinned" (Rom. 5:12).

(2) *By the disobedience of one.*—Adam, the natural and federal head of the human race, handed down to his posterity a sinful nature with the affliction of the sin principle embedded in the human blood stream.

Eve confessed that she was tempted (Gen. 3:13). She was deceived by the serpent. Adam sinned with his eyes open. He knew better. God had told him firsthand what not to do. God's message was given to Eve through Adam. Adam sinned wilfully.

Hear Paul: "And Adam was not deceived, but the woman being deceived was in the transgression" (1 Tim. 2:14). Adam sinned wilfully and maliciously and deliberately. Since that time, "all have sinned." "In Adam, all die."

"Wherefore, as by one man sin entered into the world, and death by sin" (Rom. 5:12).

5. *The Results of Sin Make Evangelism Necessary*

Sin has its payday. The wages of sin is death. All through the Bible this fact stands out. The immediate consequence of the fall is found in Genesis 3:14–19.

(1) *The curse upon the serpent.*—As a result of the first sin, a curse was placed upon the serpent. "And the Lord God said unto the serpent, Because thou hast done this, thou art cursed above all cattle, and above every beast of the field; upon thy belly shalt thou go, and dust shalt thou eat all the days of thy life: and I will put enmity between thee and the woman, and between thy seed and her seed; it shall bruise thy head, and thou shalt bruise his heel" (Gen. 3:14–15).

(2) *Sorrow to woman.*—"Unto the woman he said, I will greatly multiply thy sorrow and thy conception; in sorrow thou shalt bring forth children; and thy desire shall be to thy husband, and he shall rule over thee" (Gen. 3:16).

(3) *Wearisome labor for man.*—"And unto Adam he said, Because thou hast hearkened unto the voice of thy wife, and hast eaten of the tree, of which I commanded thee, saying, Thou shalt not eat of it: cursed is the ground for thy sake; in sorrow shalt thou eat of it all the days of thy life; thorns also and thistles shall it bring forth to thee; and thou shalt eat the herb of the field; in the sweat of thy face shalt thou eat bread, till thou return unto the ground; for out of it wast thou taken: for dust thou art, and unto dust shalt thou return. . . . Therefore the Lord God sent him forth from the garden of Eden, to till the ground from whence he was taken. So he drove out the man" (Gen. 3:17–19, 23–24).

This is no foreign language to civilized people. All of us, through everyday experiences, see all of this fulfilled because of sin. Oh, that Adam had harkened to God rather than to Eve! The prophet of God said that man's lot is but a day and full of trouble. "As for man, his days are as grass: as a flower of the field, so he flourisheth" (Psalm 103:15). It is no wonder that death continues to take its toll.

6. Evidences of Sin

On every hand one sees evidences of sin.

(1) *The Bible speaks.*—All men are sinners. The Old and New Testaments declare all men to be sinners. "There is no man that sinneth not" (1 Kings 8:46). The Preacher in Ecclesiastes says, "For there is not a just man upon earth, that doeth good, and sinneth not" (Eccl. 7:20). Isaiah the prophet declared that all men are like sheep in that they go astray (Isa. 53:6).

In the third chapter of Romans, Paul states fourteen accusations to the sinfulness of man, then emphatically declares the whole world guilty before God (Rom. 3:19). John explains why corrupt parents bear corrupt children, "That which is born of the flesh is flesh" (John 3:6). Therefore it is revealing to look at men through the revelation of the Bible: "As it is written, There is none righteous, no, not one: ... for there is no difference: for all have sinned, and come short of the glory of God" (Rom. 3:10, 22–23).

(2) *History speaks.*—Neither the Bible nor history has record of a perfect man other than Jesus Christ, but on every hand we have evidences of the sinfulness of all men. The carnal mind gives evidence that men are children of wrath because it is enmity against God. This is proved by man's neglect, his disobedience, and his direct rebellion against God's authority. The world's hatred for Christ is no less today than it was when "he came unto his own, and his own received him not" (John 1:11).

(3) *Babies reveal sinful nature.*—Still another evidence of the universality of sin is found in children even while they are tiny babes in their mothers' arms. Zophar, in trying to convince Job of his sin, said, "For vain man would be wise, though man be born like a wild ass's colt" (Job 11:12). And the psalmist declared, "The wicked are estranged from the womb: they go astray as soon as they be born, speaking lies" (Psalm 58:3).

In the Book of Wisdom we find: "Foolishness is bound in

the heart of a child; but the rod of correction shall drive it far from him" (Prov. 22:15). That explains the sudden anger of even the newborn babe. It explains the slap that the mother receives when she does not do to please the baby. That is the reason for the fit of mad temper that is evidenced in a child early in life. The sin principle is in all, and all are sinners.

(4) *Penitent sinners speak.*—Another evidence that all are sinners is the confession of sin on the part of even the best men of all times. Job was one of the best of God's followers. One day he got down in the dust of humility and confessed that he hated himself because of his sin. David cried out, "Against thee, thee only, have I sinned, and done this evil in thy sight" (Psalm 51:4). It was that same sort of feeling that caused Isaiah to confess, "Woe is me" (Isa. 6:5). Simon Peter felt so wretched over his condition that he asked the Lord to come not near him because he was a sinner.

(5) *Secular literature speaks.*—There is an old Spanish proverb that says, "There are but two good men, one dead and the other not born." Similar to the Spanish proverb is an Idaho proverb that declares that the only good Indian is a dead Indian. The Roman philosopher, Seneca, certainly hit upon a fundamental truth when he wrote, "We are all sinful; therefore whatever we blame in another, we shall find in our own bosoms." The Roman orator, Cicero, said in one of his philosophical works that nature had given us faint sparks of knowledge, but we have extinguished them with our immoralities.

Shakespeare, in his *Othello*, says, "Where's the palace whereinto foul things sometimes enter not?" He says in another of his plays, "Forbear to judge, for we are sinners all." And in another he says that God is no more responsible for the sins of man than the sun is responsible for the maggots that breed in a dead dog. Unless Shakespeare is trying to say that all men are sinners, then what could he mean?

George Eliot sets before us in her great works no perfect characters. Evidently, she, too, believed the truth of the Bible that says, "For all have sinned" (Rom. 3:23).

These and many other sources recognize the fact of sin; but for one to understand the nature, the origin, and the remedy of sin, one must go to the Bible. A New Testament church is God's agency to reveal these Bible truths to men.

7. *The Curse upon All*

Our first parents had no conception of what would take place in the history of the human race when they yielded to the tempter. Surely, the story would have been a different one if Adam and Eve had looked into the future of unborn generations and seen the results of their doings.

Sin has caused a curse upon all, for all have sinned. "And so death passed upon all men, for that all have sinned" (Rom. 5:12). "As it is written, There is none righteous, no, not one: there is none that understandeth, there is none that seeketh after God. They are all gone out of the way, they are together become unprofitable: there is none that doeth good, no, not one" (Rom. 3:10-12). "For all have sinned, and come short of the glory of God" (Rom. 3:23). "The soul that sinneth, it shall die" (Ezek. 18:4).

Sin wrecked the beautiful garden of Eden. God made man and placed him in the midst of the garden. It was the good pleasure of God to walk with Adam in the cool of the day. Sin entered the head of the family, and God was compelled to cast out the man.

Sin brought about the flood. "God saw that the wickedness of man was great in the earth, and that every imagination of the thoughts of his heart was only evil continually. And it repented the Lord that he had made man on the earth, and it grieved him at his heart. And the Lord said, I will destroy man whom I have created from the face of the earth" (Gen. 6:5-7). God called Noah to prepare the ark so that he could save the righteous from the destruction of the flood.

In Exodus 34:6-7 God warns the fathers that their children and their children's children even to the third and fourth generation would suffer the penalty of their sins. Jeremiah reminds us that God is long-suffering with lovingkindness but that he will recompense the iniquity of the fathers unto the bosom of their children after them (Jer. 32:18).

The curse upon Cain fell to his posterity. When Esau sold his birthright, he shut out all of his descendants from the covenant of promise. Achan brought the curse of death to his family because of his guilt before God. Because of David's sins the sword never departed from his house. It is unfair to coming generations for an individual to commit such evil.

Jesus told the Jews of his day that when they built the sepulchers of the prophets whom their fathers had slain, they thus acknowledged themselves sons of murderers, and that as a penalty the blood of those prophets would be required at their hands.

Oh, be careful, man, what you do, because you are not the only one who suffers when you sin. Be careful, woman, because those unborn children will share in the suffering of your iniquities. It is yet to be seen what the outcome will be of a generation of babies born to the cigarette-smoking and cocktail-drinking mothers of this age.

Sin crucified Christ. Peter pointed an accusing finger at the Sanhedrin and said, "Be it known unto you all, and to all the people of Israel, that by the name of Jesus Christ of Nazareth, whom ye crucified, whom God raised from the dead, even by him doth this man stand here before you whole" (Acts 4:10). Had it not been for sin, Jesus Christ would not have had to die. "He was bruised for our iniquities." "Christ died for our sins according to the scriptures."

Sin destroys beautiful lives. It ruins happy homes. We would never have known of a divorce court had it not been for sin. There would never have been a beautiful life wrecked and ruined had it not been for sin. Church pews would not be empty; homes would not be broken; the Lord's Day would not be desecrated; there would be no need for funeral parlors; there would be no sickness, sorrow, death, wars, or bloodshed, if man had not sinned.

There would be no need for a program of evangelism if there had been no transgression.

II. JESUS CHRIST MAKES EVANGELISM POSSIBLE

"While we were yet sinners, Christ died for us" (Rom. 5:8). This is the message of evangelism.

1. *Evangelism Was Divinely Planned*

The coming of Christ was in God's redemptive plan. God gave his Son. The only begotten Son instructed his church to be the earthly agent in the work of evangelism. The church is divine in its origin. There is no other institution like a New Testament church. God has been, and is, working at the task of growing churches. It is through churches that the good news is made known to the world. Christ, through his atoning death and resurrection, made this possible.

2. *The Good News Must Be Given to All*

There are many great words in our English language that thrill our hearts when they are mentioned. But when one seriously comes to search for the word that gladdens more hearts, puts new life and peace into more lives, and gives more hope for the future, one finds it to be "salvation." "For the grace of God that bringeth salvation hath appeared to all men" (Titus 2:11).

Without Christ there is no salvation from sin. Without a church to reveal the gospel to men, they will die in their sins. Churches have a big responsibility. They must tell the story of Jesus and his love everywhere.

3. *Salvation Is a Personal Matter*

The good news that God forgives sin is entrusted to the churches, and all true churches will continually proclaim, "He that believeth on him is not condemned." This is a matter to which each individual must give personal attention, or it would have been better not to have been born.

"For we shall all stand before the judgment seat of Christ"

(Rom. 14:10). "For it is written, As I live, saith the Lord, every knee shall bow to me, and every tongue shall confess to God. So then every one of us shall give account of himself to God" (Rom. 14:11–12). There is no way of escape. Yet "how shall they hear without a preacher? And how shall they preach, except they be sent?" (Rom. 10:14–15). Guilty, unforgiven sinners must repent or perish; saved sinners are responsible to "warn them from me," saith the Lord. The church has a big task to do.

4. Salvation Is Available for All

"And let him that heareth say, Come. And let him that is athirst come. And whosoever will, let him take the water of life freely" (Rev. 22:17). God saves a nation by saving individuals. God saves a home by saving the individuals of that home. "Ye must be born again" (John 3:7). People may come to Christ in great landslides; crowds of people may turn to the Lord at one time, but they must do it individually.

A dying man said: "Wife, all through the past you have done our churchgoing for us. You did our praying; you did our giving; you did our serving. Now that I am dying, can you stand for me?"

No, she cannot stand for him in that hour. This is an individual responsibility.

The rest of this book aims to show how the Sunday school can be made an agent for perennial evangelism.

QUESTIONS FOR REVIEW

1. Name four reasons for evangelism.
2. What is the gospel?
3. How did Christ make evangelism possible?
4. What is the place of a New Testament church in God's program of evangelism?

2

Church-Centered Evangelism

"And I say also unto thee, That thou art Peter, and upon this rock I will build my church; and the gates of hell shall not prevail against it" (Matt. 16:18).

"Then said Jesus to them again, Peace be unto you: as my Father hath sent me, even so send I you" (John 20:21).

"But ye shall receive power, after that the Holy Ghost is come upon you: and ye shall be witnesses unto me both in Jerusalem, and in all Judaea, and in Samaria, and unto the uttermost part of the earth" (Acts 1:8).

FEW PEOPLE would care to live for any length of time in a community where there is no church. A New Testament church is God's instrument to promote evangelism. It is the best influence in the community.

New Testament churches hold in their grasp the destiny of the world. They are entrusted with, and responsible for, sharing with the nations the gospel of the Lord Jesus Christ. The Commission was given to the church. Christ is holding his church responsible for "discipling the nations." If New Testament churches fail Christ in the work of evangelism, they fail in their chief business. And no other institution can do for evangelism what God intends for the church to do. The churches have a monopoly of evangelism.

I. THE FOUNDER OF NEW TESTAMENT CHURCHES WAS "THE EVANGELIST"

Jesus earned the title "the Evangelist."

1. *Jesus Was the Friend of Sinners*

Jesus Christ spent his life here on earth in the interest of lost people. It was for the salvation of the souls and lives of lost people that Jesus was chiefly concerned. He came not to call the righteous but sinners to repentance. He came that all might have life and that in abundance. To this end he spent his time preaching, teaching, and healing. His compassion for the multitudes, along with a passion to do the will of his Father, moved him to do all that he did.

2. *Evangelism Was the Natural Thing with Jesus*

Jesus lived evangelism. He was really God and he was really man. God is love, and Jesus Christ, the God-man, could do nothing less than love a lost world. To love a lost world as his Father did, he must be about his Father's business. He worked miracles in the interest of saving people. His nature would not allow him to do less. He was and is Deity. It was only natural for him to restore things to their proper order. This accounts for the miracles of Jesus.

3. *All That Jesus Did Was for Evangelism*

Jesus was, and is, life; therefore death could not stay in his presence. Diseased and broken bodies were made whole when they came into contact with him, for he is the Great Physician. What Jesus did for the body of man, he did in the interest of his soul.

As "the Evangelist" Jesus went about doing good. He had evangelism on his heart, as it was and is on the heart of God. Jesus talked about it. He did it. He taught it to his followers. He practiced it every day. This is what he spent his time doing.

Jesus died that the work of evangelism might be possible. He would have his followers who make up his churches do nothing less than think, live, talk, and practice evangelism. This means that every Christian should be vitally concerned about the work of evangelism.

II. The Church Was Instituted for Evangelism

The idea of a New Testament church was conceived in the heart of God. The church had its origin in Jesus Christ. Man has conceived the idea of other institutions, but not a New Testament church. It is unique.

1. Christ Its Founder

No lesser personage than Jesus Christ is the Founder of the church. He said, "I will build my church" (Matt. 16:18). The Designer, the Architect, and the Builder is Christ. The first believers, Jesus took as living stones (1 Peter 2:4-5), and said, "I will build my church" (Matt. 16:18). He, of course, is "the chief corner stone" (Eph. 2:20). John said, "All things were made by him; and without him was not any thing made that was made" (John 1:3). This same Christ said, "Preach the gospel to every creature."

2. Christ Its Head

Christ is the head of the church. He instituted it and he alone has the right to say what its main business is. When Jesus Christ speaks, the last word is said. "Hear ye him" is the admonition of the Father. He said, "All power is given unto me in heaven and in earth. Go ye . . ." (Matt. 28:18-19). Christ loved the church and gave himself for it. He holds the exclusive right to be the head of the church.

3. Christ Its Sustainer

Jesus Christ is not only the Founder, he is the Foundation and the chief Cornerstone of the church. He holds things together. "And he is before all things, and by him all things consist" (Col. 1:17). Only Jesus Christ could say, "And, lo, I am with you alway" (Matt. 28:20).

III. Evangelism Is Dependent upon the Church

The evangel is the good news. An evangelist is one who tells the good news—the gospel story. Evangelism is the proclamation of the gospel to the end that the soul and life of the lost sinner who hears it might be saved, conserved, and made useful.

1. *The Gospel Has Been Committed to the Church*

John the Baptist expressed the gospel thus: "Behold the Lamb of God, which taketh away the sin of the world" (John 1:29). Simon Peter said, "There is none other name under heaven given among men, whereby we must be saved (Acts 4:12). Paul said, "This is a faithful saying, and worthy of all acceptation, that Christ Jesus came into the world to save sinners; of whom I am chief" (1 Tim. 1:15). Jesus said to Nicodemus, "For God so loved the world, that he gave his only begotten Son, that whosoever believeth in him should not perish, but have everlasting life" (John 3:16). This good news has been committed to the church for its proclamation to the world (Matt. 28:18–20). If the church fails, then Christ has no other plan.

2. *The Sunday School Is the Church Organized for Evangelism*

The Sunday school in a New Testament church, if organized to do so, can find the people of a community and enlist them in Bible study. In and through such Bible study, hearts are prepared to receive the Christ of the gospel. Churches that have utilized the Sunday school in evangelism have had continuous, fruitful results. New Testament evangelism is perennial. This is the chief business of every church, and it is possible through the proper use of the Sunday school.

3. *Yet Some Communities Have No Church*

"How shall they believe in him of whom they have not heard? and how shall they hear without a preacher? And how shall they preach, except they be sent?" (Rom. 10:14–15). A New Testament church within practical reach of every person is the answer. Existing churches are responsible to help build churches in every community.

IV. FIRST-CENTURY EVANGELISM WAS CHURCH CENTERED

The New Testament record reveals that the churches of the first century were centers of all evangelistic activities. Evangelism that has no regard for the place of a New Testament church cannot prove fruitful and lasting.

Perhaps the best record available of New Testament evangelism in action is the Acts of the Apostles. A careful study of this book under the direction of the pastor would be of immense value to any church. The work of evangelism is a big task. One cannot do it alone; there must be co-operation. This is a work for organized effort—the work of a church.

1. *The Jerusalem Church*

The church at Jerusalem, empowered by the Holy Spirit, became so concerned about the main work of a church that 3,000 souls were saved one day (Acts 2:41). On another occasion, "many of them which heard the word believed; and the number of the men was about five thousand" (Acts 4:4). Because of the evangelistic fervor of the people, the number of disciples multiplied until it was necessary for the church in Jerusalem to increase its organization (Acts 6:1-7).

Evangelism must have something for people after they are saved from sin. Nothing but a church can stabilize, conserve, and utilize saved people. A Sunday school should furnish a place of service and development for every member of the church.

2. *The Church at Antioch*

It was during a prayer meeting that the Holy Spirit commissioned the church at Antioch to send Paul and Barnabas on a far-reaching quest for souls (Acts 13:2). The church at Antioch undertook to carry out the Great Commission. They felt their responsibility, not only at home, but also around the world. This is New Testament evangelism. It includes "Jerusalem," but it takes in "regions beyond" as well. Bible teaching by Spirit-led teachers in a Sunday school that has a growing, vital program bears the same fruit today.

As members are led to apply the Bible truths to their own lives, they feel God's call to be missionaries at home and abroad.

3. *Other Evidences*

From house to house first-century Christians went. That is not all: "They that were scattered abroad went every where preaching the word" (Acts 8:4). These were church people, doing church work. Jesus "went about." Those who followed him while he was in the flesh tried to imitate his example. Not all the work of a church can be done within the church walls.

A church today is following the New Testament pattern when it uses its Sunday school organization to send people afield to take a census, and later to follow up the census with purposeful ministry to each individual for whom the church is responsible.

V. HINDRANCES TO EVANGELISM APPEAR IN SOME CHURCHES

The work of evangelism is vital to the life and program of a church. Yet some churches have so much interference that the fires of evangelism burn dimly. No perfection of Sunday school organization can make a church a power for evangelism while certain hindrances are permitted to remain.

1. *Unchristian Conduct*

Shabby, shoddy living on the part of all too many professed Christians hinders the progress of the gospel. Unchristian conduct dishonors Christ, disgusts lost people, and causes the witness of the church to lose its power. Christians with unconfessed sin in their lives do not win people to Christ. Compassion for souls is no companion to secret sins. When part of "the body" is unfit, the whole is hindered.

2. *Lukewarm Spirit*

Indifference or unconcern of Christians hinders a successful program of evangelism in a church. Evangelism cannot thrive in the soil of complacency. A church with a wide-awake, forward-moving, evangelistic spirit can trample underfoot the unconcern of some of its members. But the ascended, resurrected Lord spoke hard words of criticism to the indifferent, unconcerned, complacent church at Laodicea (Rev. 3:15-17).

3. *Disunity in the Church Family*

Divisions in a church will chill and kill an evangelistic spirit. The program of evangelism cannot thrive where a house is divided against itself. Divisions breed hatred instead of love, jealousy instead of concern and compassion.

4. *The Wrong Spirit*

Too often dissatisfied, disgruntled church members hinder the evangelistic spirit and progress in churches. Many people who should be hot on the trail of souls, winning them to Christ, instead hinder those who would be after souls and thus dishonor the cause of Christ.

5. *Misplaced Emphasis*

Churches that major on minors will never have the genuine compassion for souls that they should have. When priority is given to anything other than reaching, teaching, winning, and developing people; when the major emphasis from the pulpit is on lecturing instead of preaching the gospel; when good deeds are emphasized instead of repentance; physical needs rather than spiritual; recreational programs at the expense of Bible study and prayer, the evangelistic fervor will not rise to high tide.

6. *The Wrong Conception of the Work of the Pastor*

Some churches use pastors for "flunkies" instead of giving them a free hand in the ministry of the Word and prayer. How can such men be great preachers of the Word when they spend their time with minor details? Too many give themselves to piddling instead of soul-winning. The Great Commission calls for conquest. The pastor is to be out front leading his church in this great advance.

No pastor multiplies himself more effectively than when he leads his church in a program of Sunday school work which enlists and trains numbers of his members in service. Happy the pastor who, through an enlarged Sunday school organization, puts many people to work, and so multiplies the number of human outlets through which the Holy Spirit operates in the church.

7. *Failure to Give the Holy Spirit His Rightful Place*

When the Holy Spirit is not fully recognized and given his rightful place, major emphasis will not be given to the work of evangelism. Spirit-filled men and women are soul-winners. They have compassion for those who are without Christ. Such people help their church to do the work of evangelism.

8. *Sunday School Not Fully Used*

Some churches have never had a clear vision of the opportunities for evangelism through the use of the Sunday school; therefore perennial evangelism is impossible. Occasional efforts to find, win to Christ, and enlist people bring about some victories. But churches that make proper use of the Sunday school see fruitful results week by week.

A perennial program of sowing and reaping for the Lord is New Testament evangelism. Anything short of this will dishonor Christ. The Sunday school, when properly organized and used, is the best-known channel available for reaching out in a perennial effort to evangelize the people of a community. And a warm, vital, Spirit-directed program of Bible study in the Sunday school is the best cure for the hindrances in evangelism which have been named.

VI. An Unevangelistic Church Dishonors God

The purpose of New Testament churches is evangelism. For no other reason do they exist.

1. *To Fail in Evangelism Is to Be a Failure*

If and when a church ceases to be evangelistic, it dishonors God. "Ichabod"—no glory—had as well be written over the church door. A New Testament church is a "lamp-stand" to hold forth the Light of the world. To fail at this point is to fail everywhere. Nothing can take the place of the work in evangelism.

2. Failure to Evangelize Forfeits the Right to Exist

Jesus said to the church at Ephesus, a church that had left its first love: "Repent, . . . or else I will come unto thee quickly, and will remove thy candlestick" (Rev. 2:5). To Pergamos, whose witness had been silenced because of sin in the congregation, Jesus said: "Repent; or else I will come unto thee quickly, and will fight against them with the sword of my mouth" (Rev. 2:16). To Sardis, who had a name that she lived yet she was dead, Jesus said: "Repent" (Rev. 3:3). The message of the one who has "all power" to the churches of Asia and to all churches that have ceased to put first things first, is *Repent*. Such churches dishonor God. His denunciation will be forthcoming.

VII. We Come to Some Inescapable Conclusions

Every Christian should give his best through his church to the cause of evangelism. Everyone who properly visualizes the call of the multitudes will be busy at the task of reaching them. Every well-informed Christian will see that the most effective channel for church-centered evangelism is a functioning Sunday school program.

1. The World Cannot Get Along Without New Testament Churches

The local church is God's instrument in this age to promote his program of evangelism. The local church that does not major on evangelism is not New Testament in practice. Evangelism that does not enlist new converts in local church membership does not go far enough. The program of evangelism that emphasizes winning souls only is incomplete. Lives as well as souls must be saved. The work of evangelism is responsible for the salvation of the whole man. This is the type of evangelism which results when a church majors on using its Sunday school for doing the main work of the church.

2. *Every Community Should Be Churched*

Southern Baptists are in line with New Testament evangelism when they endeavor to put a New Testament church within easy reach of everyone.

The apostle Paul gathered together the people in each community whom he won to Christ, and organized them into a church. He later visited or wrote letters to most of the churches to make sure of their continued growth in grace and spiritual development.

Churches today must continue this sort of work. Failure to start a church in a community is to leave that community to decay. The work of a church in a community, like leaven, continues to leaven the lump. It is a constant force for good.

3. *Church-centered Evangelism Is the Key*

Permanency in evangelism depends upon the church. All outside efforts at evangelism must depend upon churches to take over and stabilize, or there will be no lasting, fruitful results. The Sunday school is the greatest evangelistic agency of a church. It assures permanency in evangelism. The pastor who realizes his opportunity through the Sunday school, and rightly uses it, is wise indeed. The program of Christian education in any church, if not geared to evangelism, will prove to be a hindrance. Every agency of a church should contribute to the evangelistic endeavor of that church. One that does not has no right to exist. It is, or should be, all for evangelism.

4. *Church-centered Evangelism Has No Local Bounds*

A church, to do the task that New Testament evangelism requires, cannot be satisfied within the walls of the church building. The people, many of them, will not, of their own accord, come to church. A church must go beyond her doors, out into the "outreaches" after the people.

The business of the church is to proclaim God's remedy

for sin to sinners everywhere. Every time this is done, some will accept it. Jesus said, "And I, if I be lifted up from the earth, will draw all men unto me" (John 12:32). It is the business of every Christian and every church to lift up Christ. A New Testament church is Christ's agency to proclaim the gospel message, not only to the people in the community, but to the whole world.

5. The Message of the Church Is the Hope of the World

Our hope for a world such as ours is for New Testament churches to "go . . . make disciples." In what better way can one spend his time? What can one do that will pay bigger dividends? What will bring peace and joy to individuals, homes, communities, and nations, like the gospel of Christ brings when it is properly proclaimed?

The pulpit must magnify the love and compassion of God for sinners as it is revealed in Christ. God's prophet must have a vision of the hotness of hell to which lost, unredeemed men go when they die. To know the worth of a soul, the pastor must realize the price God paid to become the Saviour of man. This will help to keep the preacher's heart hot. Everyone needs to hear Jesus ask, "What shall it profit a man, if he shall gain the whole world, and lose his own soul?" (Mark 8:36).

Preacher and people must go and sit where lost people sit before they really grieve over their undone condition (Ezek. 3:15). "Where there is no vision, the people perish" (Prov. 29:18). Genuine concern must be preceded by a vision of the conditions and needs of people. There would be twenty-five thousand new missions opened next Sunday if all the pastors and deacons of the Southern Baptist Convention would go and sit where the unreached multitudes sit.

6. Evangelism Is Not Optional—It Is Imperative

The evangelistic church, with an evangelistic program, motivated by an evangelistic spirit, will go everywhere preaching the gospel. Every church will be an honor to God and an instrument in bringing salvation to lost men, all of which brings rejoicing in heaven and on earth. The church that loses its passion for souls is headed for the "dry rot."

Pulpits need to be filled with men who have a passion for souls. Moses, who was willing to be blotted out of God's book for the salvation of his people, had it. Jeremiah, who wished that his head were waters and his eyes a fountain of tears, if by weeping he could save an apostate people, had passion for souls. Paul, who was willing to be accursed from Christ if at such cost his kinsmen according to the flesh could be saved, had it.

All too many pastors and churches have been tempted to give their time and effort to secondary things instead of majoring on evangelism. Many Sunday school teachers give more time to planning and sponsoring picnics and frolics for their classes than they do to enlisting and winning lost pupils to Christ. It has been proved beyond any doubt that when the preacher from the pulpit, the teacher in the classroom, the Christian in the place of business will reason, as did Paul, of righteousness, temperance, and judgment, sinners will tremble.

When New Testament churches preach and teach the simple gospel of Christ, fervently, constantly, and believingly, it is still "the power of God unto salvation to everyone that believeth." Stay on the main line and great numbers will turn to the Lord. "And the Lord added to the church daily such as should be saved" (Acts 2:47).

Evangelism through the use of the Sunday school, as is advocated in this book, is church centered. It is perennial. It involves the whole personality of each individual. It is the most effective and substantial program of evangelism known. It is based on sound, New Testament principles.

QUESTIONS FOR REVIEW

1. What is the relationship of Jesus to a New Testament church?
2. What part does the church have in the work of evangelism?
3. What is meant by church-centered evangelism?
4. Name eight hindrances to the work of evangelism.

3

A Church Equipped for Evangelism

"And Jesus came and spake unto them, saying, All power is given unto me in heaven and in earth. Go ye therefore, and teach all nations, baptizing them in the name of the Father, and of the Son, and of the Holy Ghost: teaching them to observe all things whatsoever I have commanded you: and, lo, I am with you alway, even unto the end of the world" (Matt. 28:18-20).

ETERNITY ALONE can reveal what a New Testament church means to the people who avail themselves of its blessings. Eye hath not seen nor hath ear heard the full value that Jesus Christ put on a New Testament church. The human mind cannot fathom the true worth of a church.

What is there about the church that Christ could so love it as to give himself for it? What of an institution or organism about which the Son of God said, "The gates of hell shall not prevail against it"?

One might well ask, "What is a church?" Many and varied are the ideas about a church. The only safe thing for one to do is to turn to the trustworthy source—the New Testament —for the correct answer.

A New Testament church is a local assembly of "called-out" ones, each of whom is a regenerated, scripturally baptized believer in Jesus Christ. They are joined together as a body of believers in Christ, to carry out his commands set forth in the Great Commission (Matt. 28:19-20). A New Testament church is obligated to carry out the marching orders of its Commander in chief. There is work to be done at home and around the world.

I. The Church Is Commissioned to Evangelize

Jesus has stated the program of evangelism that he expects every church to follow.

1. *Jesus Christ Clearly Defined the Task of a Church*

The marching order of the Commander in chief, the Founder and Head of New Testament churches, is "make disciples, baptize, teach, utilize." Surely, no one who has been blood-bought and redeemed could do less than follow the orders of the One who redeemed him.

Some so-called New Testament churches go a year at a time without locating and winning one soul to Christ. Of course, there is more to evangelism than winning the soul to Christ; but where people work at the task of evangelism, souls are going to be saved. Christians who do not point others to Christ are not growing in the Christian graces.

The chief business of a Christian is to produce fruit. The fruit of one Christian is another. Could it also be that the fruit of a church is another church? Like produces like. Saved people are under obligation by divine compulsion to be soul-winners.

Churches are to baptize, teach, and utilize. Disciples are liabilities until they are assimilated. It takes a worthy church program to assimilate properly new converts. The Sunday school should not be overlooked in this program. It is available and adequate. When it is used to the best advantage, fruitful results will follow.

Pastors and churches that use the Sunday school testify to its adequacy. No one could doubt that the Bible-teaching agency of a New Testament church has been given of God. It should be utilized in his program. It has in it the soul-winners; the souls to be won; the Bible, which is the sword of the Spirit; and the proper organization for winning the lost to Christ and utilizing the saved.

What better way is available to a church to teach the gospel than through the proper use of the Sunday school? Of course, the Sunday school does not take the place of pulpit preaching and teaching, but when rightly used, the Sunday school will put more people into the worship services. One of our seminary professors often said, "Teaching and preaching are not two separate services, but two halves of a whole, and neither is complete without the other."

2. Figures of Speech Reveal the Purpose of a Church

A careful study of the different terms used in the New Testament to describe a church should help us to understand its purpose and work and lead us to give ourselves to growing New Testament churches.

(1) *A lampstand.*—John, in the Revelation, uses the term "lampstand" to convey his idea of a New Testament church. Candelabras and lampstands give no light, but when functioning properly, they hold forth light. A church is not the light, but it holds forth the Light, which is Christ. The church is to lift up Jesus Christ, who in turn will light this world, for he said, "I am the light of the world" (John 8:12).

(2) *A family.*—Believers are brethren, heirs of God, and joint heirs with Christ. The Scriptures speak of a church as "the household of God" and "the household of faith." This reveals another angle of the purpose and place of a church in the redemptive plan of God for the ages. No one deserves the glorious privilege of this sacred relationship; yet it pleased God to make it possible.

(3) *The bride of Christ.*—John referred to the church as "the bride of Christ." What a beautiful picture! "The Spirit and the bride say, Come" (Rev. 22:17). This figure of speech magnifies the evangelistic purpose of a church, which is the primal purpose of a church.

(4) *The body of Christ.*—The church is spoken of in the Bible as "the body of Christ." "Ye are the body of Christ, and members in particular" (1 Cor. 12:27).

(5) *God's building.*—"Ye are God's building" (1 Cor. 3:9). Simon Peter spoke of the church as a "spiritual house" made of living stones (1 Peter 2:4–5). How could one misunderstand such graphic language? "Know ye not that ye are the temple of God, and that the Spirit of God

dwelleth in you?" (1 Cor. 3:16). What a sacred relationship!

Dr. Charles E. Jefferson contrasts an audience with a church, in his book *The Building of the Church*. "An audience," he said, "is a crowd, a church is a family. An audience is a gathering, a church is a fellowship. An audience is a collection, the church is an organism. An audience is a heap of stones, a church is a temple. Preachers are ordained, not to attract an audience, but to build a church."[1]

II. THE CHURCH IS EQUIPPED FOR ITS WORK

The church is not left in the world to do its task alone. Christ has empowered and equipped his church to carry out that which he has commissioned her to do.

A Sunday school, properly functioning, practically insures that a church will fulfil all the figures named. It will serve to hold forth the word of light to more people; to deepen fellowship within the family of God; to echo and re-echo the invitation, come; to keep the body of Christ in good health; and to add living stores to the spiritual temple.

1. *The Church Has the Message*

"And [Jesus] said unto them, Thus it is written, and thus it behoved Christ to suffer, and to rise from the dead the third day: and that repentance and remission of sins should be preached in his name among all nations, beginning at Jerusalem" (Luke 24:46-47). "For God sent not his Son into the world to condemn the world; but that the world through him might be saved. He that believeth on him is not condemned: but he that believeth not is condemned already, because he hath not believed in the name of the only begotten Son of God" (John 3:17-18).

(1) *The ordinance of baptism visualizes the message.*— Baptism is an ordinance given to the church by Jesus Christ. Its mode portrays burial and resurrection. It visualizes what has taken place in the life of the believer at conversion—

[1] Jefferson, Charles E., *The Building of the Church* (New York: Macmillan Company, 1910), p. 67. Used by permission (out of print).

death to sin and spiritual resurrection from this death by the power of the Holy Spirit. It is a picture of the future resurrection of the believer's body. Again, baptism pictures a historical fact—the death, burial, and resurrection of Jesus Christ.

Baptism does not save anybody. It is an outward evidence of inward confession of sin, of faith in Christ, and of acceptance of the gospel plan of salvation (Mark 1:5; Matt. 3:5-6; Acts 2:41; 8:12). Baptism is the doorway into a New Testament church. It has no saving merit, neither does it impart any means of grace to the sinner.

It is the responsibility of a New Testament church, as part of its program of perennial evangelism, to lead those who accept Christ as Saviour to follow him in baptism. That the Sunday school is an effective agency in doing this has been demonstrated by the many churches which have used their Sunday schools as a means of maintaining a ratio of one baptism for every eight church members.

(2) *The ordinance of the Lord's Supper sets forth the message.*—The Lord's Supper is one of two perpetual ordinances given by the Lord to his churches. Jesus instituted the Memorial Supper before his death on Calvary. He would have his followers remember his death; therefore he left this memorial. He used two symbols to represent his body and his blood. "This," he said, "do in remembrance of me. . . . For as often as ye eat this bread, and drink this cup, ye do shew the Lord's death till he come" (1 Cor. 11:24, 26).

The purpose of the Supper, therefore, is to proclaim the Lord's death till he comes. Baptism pictures the burial and resurrection of our Lord—thus the whole gospel message is visualized in the two ordinances.

2. *Leadership Is Available for the Task*

The New Testament church did not require much organization in its infancy. Pastors were the only officers at first. The early churches had several pastors. In Ephesians 4:11 Paul says that Christ gave apostles, prophets, evangelists, pastors, and teachers. The implication is that these leaders were placed in the churches as needed. We know that when the need arose, God gave other helpers, who later came to be known as deacons.

No one would doubt that the Sunday school, Training Union, and other agencies belong in a New Testament church today in order to meet specific needs that have come with growth. There is a conviction among many that should other needs arise God will reveal to his people other agencies or organizations necessary to meet such needs.

3. The Church Has Authority and Power for the Task

"But ye shall receive power, after that the Holy Ghost is come upon you: and ye shall be witnesses unto me both in Jerusalem, and in all Judaea, and in Samaria, and unto the uttermost part of the earth" (Acts 1:8). "And, lo, I am with you alway" (Matt. 28:20). Herein lies the authority for churches.

Jesus Christ is the head of the church. He is the chief Cornerstone. Christ identifies himself with his church. When Paul was persecuting the church, Jesus said, "Saul, Saul, why persecutest thou me?"

Christ commissioned the church. The marching orders of the church came from the one who has all authority. Christ empowers the church. The source of power in a church is unlimited, if and when conditions are met.

Christ issued the blueprints for the church. The Bible is the chart and compass for those who would build and grow New Testament churches (1 Cor. 3:9–10; Eph. 2:20–22; 1 Peter 2:4–5).

III. THE NEW TESTAMENT PROVIDES A PATTERN TO FOLLOW

It has been stated that a New Testament church is a local assembly of regenerated, scripturally baptized believers in Christ, joined together for the purpose of carrying the gospel into all the world. This means that a church is to begin in its "Jerusalem" and go to the ends of the earth with the gospel of the Lord Jesus Christ.

Many congregations that call themselves New Testament

churches are not doing much about the main task of a church. True New Testament churches prove themselves to be missionary. The whole program of such a church is centered in the work of New Testament evangelism. A careful study of the book of Acts will reveal some important facts about a New Testament church. Every church that claims to be after the New Testament pattern would do well to measure itself in the light of the teachings of the Acts of the Apostles.

1. Democratic and Autonomous in Government

Democracy in its purest form is found in a New Testament church. When an assembly fails to follow this pattern, then it has sidestepped the teachings of the Bible concerning church government.

(1) *Vacancy filled.*—The vacancy left by Judas was filled by the people. The first chapter of the book of Acts gives light on the subject. Simon Peter stood and told the group that the vacancy left by Judas should be filled, and mentioned some qualifications for the one who should be chosen. Peter did not fill the vacancy himself. He brought the matter before the people. They evidently studied the membership, because two names were suggested. From the two nominated, one was chosen by casting lots, as was the custom of voting in that day. Prayer was offered before lots were cast. The lot fell on Matthias (Acts 1:15–26).

If a church today would use its Sunday school in the ministry of perennial evangelism, that church must see to it that vacancies are filled and the expansion provided for in the Sunday school organization.

(2) *Helpers elected.*—In Acts, chapter 6, we find the church in Jerusalem in business session selecting from among the membership seven men who could qualify for the service that was to be rendered. This was the action of the church, carried out at the suggestion of the apostles. Here we find a pure democracy.

There is no place in a New Testament church for a dictatorship. A true New Testament church is democratic in government. Let no one rule and ruin the church of God! The only head of the church is Jesus Christ. Give him his rightful place in the church and church-centered evangelism will prevail. He will lead the church to find, enlist, and elect a sufficient corps of God-called, Spirit-selected Sunday school workers to form the vanguard of an aggressive evangelistic program.

(3) *Advice from mother church.*—Churches may co-operate with and assist one another. In the fifteenth chapter of the book of Acts, we find that the church in Antioch was democratic in government. Sinners were being saved by grace through faith. Certain Judaizers, who would hinder salvation by grace, came from Jerusalem. They disturbed the people. The Antioch church sent a committee to Jerusalem to confer with the mother church in the matter.

When the conference was assembled in Jerusalem, it pleased the elders and the whole church to send only suggestions to the church in Antioch (Acts 15:22–29). Neither of these churches had any jurisdiction over the other. Advice was sought and given, but the local group had to make the final decision.

Our program of co-operative effort through the associational organization stems from this pattern.

(4) *Each an independent group.*—A New Testament church is an independent body, and "everybody is somebody." Each local assembly is a separate and distinct body of believers, responsible only to God. The Bible speaks of "the church" here and "the church" there. "Salute the brethren which are in Laodicea, and Nymphas, and the church which is in his house" (Col. 4:15).

Every member of the congregation can and should have a voice and vote on all matters of business and policy transacted by a New Testament church. One person has as much right to freedom of expression as another in a church. Neither pastors nor deacons have any authority by virtue of their office, except as the church delegates authority to them. Each individual member has the right to vote on all matters that pertain to the life or the affairs of a church.

Each should be given this privilege. When this procedure is practiced, usually the people are satisfied and things go well.

2. For Saved People Only

All regenerated believers in Christ, and only such, should belong to a church.

The corollary of this principle is that every member of the church should be serving as a part of the body of Christ. A church is strengthened in the whole program of kingdom work when the Sunday school is so used as to furnish a place of service for every church member.

The Lord adds to the church. The New Testament church is the place for membership and service of those who have been saved. "Then they that gladly received his word were baptized: . . . And the Lord added to the church daily such as should be saved" (Acts 2:41, 47). Saved people, and only those saved, should belong to a New Testament church. The only organization of a New Testament church which lost people may, without reserve, be invited to join is the Sunday school. A functioning Sunday school is the arm of the church reaching out to bring the unsaved under the influence of Bible study, and thus increasing the likelihood that they will be saved and become church members.

3. Right on the Money Question

Church members are in possession of enough of God's money to do everything that God expects, at home and abroad. All too few of them voluntarily bring it into his storehouse.

The early New Testament church was right on money matters. "And all that believed were together, and had all things common; and sold their possessions and goods, and parted them to all men, as every man had need. . . . And the multitude of them that believed were of one heart and of one soul: neither said any of them that ought of the things which he possessed was his own; but they had all things common" (Acts 2:44-45; 4:32). This explains many things.

Christians are stewards of their possessions. And most of them will get right in regard to this matter if and when they are fully informed. So great was the spirit and liberality of Joses, a Levite of Cyprus, that he was called by a new name, Barnabas, meaning "the son of consolation."

There is room for improvement at this point in many churches today. People must be informed about their Christian duty. The right kind of program helps develop Christians in stewardship. The Sunday school is valuable at this point when properly used. The Bible-centered curriculum of the Sunday school has stewardship interwoven in all its teaching. The organization of the units of the Sunday school furnishes direction for each individual to learn stewardship through practice.

4. Right Emphasis on the Word of God

After deacons were elected, the church put the major emphasis where it belonged. The apostles said: "We will give ourselves continually to prayer, and to the ministry of the word" (Acts 6:4). It is no wonder that "the word of God increased; and the number of the disciples multiplied in Jerusalem greatly" (Acts 6:7).

It is easy to understand why souls were saved when Peter preached. The power of God accompanied his message. Peter's message was "Jesus Christ." To him there was only one way out for sinners. Jesus is the answer. Peter preached Jesus Christ and him crucified as the only remedy for sinful men.

The preachers of the first century were on fire for God. They spent much time in prayer and Bible study. In a genuine New Testament church there will be this sort of preaching today. Preachers should not be turned aside from preaching the whole counsel of God. Preachers must "warn the people for God."

A functioning Sunday school promotes Bible-centered preaching. The people who attend Sunday school are "readied" for the preaching hour by their period of Bible study, and they are stimulated to attend through the efforts of an active class and department organization.

5. *It Reached Out to New Areas*

Philip went to Samaria and preached Christ to the people there. Multitudes were saved. The Holy Spirit sent Philip down to the highway and joined him to the chariot of an Ethiopian eunuch, and he preached Jesus to him (Acts 8:35).

Wherever Christ is preached, sinners are saved, for "the gospel of Christ . . . is the power of God unto salvation." Christ is the center of all New Testament preaching. He is the one message. Is it any wonder that the eunuch asked Philip to baptize him? The gospel had been preached; the Holy Spirit had done his work; the sinner had repented and confessed his faith in Christ. It was time for a baptismal service. Evidently the church in Jerusalem had commissioned deacon Philip to baptize converts into their fellowship. And the commission failed to stipulate color or kind.

6. *Every Christian a Witness*

It seems that every first-century follower of Christ accepted his responsibility as a witness to the grace of God. The chief concern and business of every Christian was to give the gospel to someone else. Acts 8:4 says, "They that were scattered abroad went every where preaching the word." Christians who were scattered by persecution preached Jesus Christ wherever they went.

The apostles remained in Jerusalem, but the followers of Jesus counted it a privilege to preach Jesus everywhere they went. Every Christian is duly responsible to do this sort of witnessing. Men, women, and all who knew Christ told about him. If churches are as evangelistic as they should be, then, not only will the preachers preach Jesus Christ, but every member will also do the same.

The program of a growing Sunday school ensures that its members shall be sent afield everywhere to find lost people, witness to them, and bring them in to classes where they are exposed to the word of God in the hands of Spirit-led teachers. Is it any wonder that we win eighty of the lost people whom we enrol and hold in our Sunday schools for every one lost person whom we win apart from this ministry?

7. A Praying Church

The church in Jerusalem tarried at the command of Jesus. They prayed while they waited. After they had prayed, the place was shaken where they were assembled (Acts 4:31).

The early Christians felt their need of God. They did not have any "pull" with the city officials, but they had "power" with God. They received an answer when they prayed. James had been put to death (Acts 12:2); Simon Peter was in prison; but the little Jerusalem church was in prayer (Acts 12:5), and God heard and answered.

The church in Jerusalem literally prayed Peter out of jail. God delivered him and sent him to the place where the prayer was being offered. Those praying were surprised. They had prayed, believing; yet they were amazed. God had answered their prayers while they were praying.

Back in the days of the depression a college friend of mine told me that on Christmas Eve, without a penny in the house and with two small boys looking for Santa Claus, he and his wife had prayed almost all the morning. Just before time for the bank to close, he got up off his knees and started to the bank to see if he could get as much as one dollar. But before he got off the college campus, a Christian man met him and gave him five dollars—a gift for Christmas.

While my friend was praying, God was at work answering the prayer. That was the very thing that happened to the Jerusalem church. It would happen again and again if we "tarried" in prayer as we should for the advancement of God's work.

God has not changed. Is yours a New Testament church? Is the power of God felt in it? Churches have prayed jails open. They have prayed men out of jail. No less power is available for every church today. Jesus Christ is the same yesterday, today, and forever. Why are some churches so powerless?

8. A Soul-winning Church

A New Testament church is a soul-winning church. The record reveals that 120 Christians won 3,000 people to Christ in one day (Acts 2:41). It takes twenty Southern Baptists a whole year to win one soul to Christ. What is wrong? Why are we so helpless? Why do we not have more people saved in our services? Some churches each year baptize one person for every six or eight church members. Other churches baptize none in a year. Is such a church doing the work of evangelism? A church centered in the work of evangelism will correct such failure.

Perennial evangelism is possible in every church. In the book of Acts we find churches winning people to Christ every day. A program of perennial evangelism through the proper use of the Sunday school will reach people daily for Christ. It seems that the Sunday school at work comes near the New Testament pattern.

All the Christians of the first century thought it their business to win others to Christ. Those closest to the cross felt this responsibility. The Sunday school today keeps people constantly after the lost. Free leaflets for a program of perennial evangelism through the Sunday school are available at the Baptist Sunday School Board, Nashville 3, Tennessee.

The Sunday school is adequate for soul-winning because it is organized for the work of evangelism. Its organization is made up of the best soul-winners in the church. Its constituency includes many who are lost and need to be won to Christ. Evidently God gave the Sunday school to the church for this particular task.

9. A Missionary Church

"And that repentance and remission of sins should be preached in his name among all nations, beginning at Jerusalem" (Luke 24:47). The missionary spirit will prevail in a New Testament church. Christians of the first century were missionaries. The church will have the world on its heart if it is patterned after the New Testament. Jesus has outlined the task. The world is the field. We are our brothers' keepers. We have brothers all over the world.

"Make disciples" is the divine command. The anti-missionary spirit is anti-New Testament. Followers of the Lord Jesus will not let the local field take up all the time, money, and prayers. The entire world should be on our hearts.

First-century Christians began in Jerusalem, but they did not stop until all Asia had heard the message. The Scriptures say that the Word of God increased. People realized their stewardship responsibility for sharing the Word of God and did their best to discharge it. Christians were living epistles. Baptist churches today have the same privilege and responsibility. A program is available to those desiring it.

Missions is the test of a missionary church. A sign "Missionary Baptist Church" over a church door does not guarantee that the church is missionary. What is the real test? Dr. A. J. Gordon, of Boston, so instilled the missionary spirit into the people of the church of which he was pastor that, the first Lord's Day after his death, they decided that the way to make their pastor's first Lord's Day in heaven what he would desire would be to make their missionary offering that day the largest in history. They did.

A survey would reveal that too little is included in many church budgets for real missionary work. The church that does not have the world at heart is not a New Testament church. The heart's desire of every pastor should be that, someday, somewhere, somehow, God would help him develop a real missionary church—a church that actually believes in missions.

If one believes in missions, one will practice missions. Oh, for the day to come when Southern Baptists prove their love to God through a worldwide program of evangelism! A church can improve its stewardship enlistment program many-fold through the right use of the Sunday school. The Bible is filled with the message of stewardship and missions.

Its regular systematic study in the Sunday school will be used of the Holy Spirit to give Christians a vision and a sense of obligation in respect to missions.

IV. FOLLOWING THE NEW TESTAMENT PATTERN BRINGS RESULTS

A church which is using its Sunday school and its other organizations to maintain work on "the main line" of perennial evangelism will see results.

1. Sinners Saved

"The Son of man is come to seek and to save that which was lost" (Luke 19:10). Perennial evangelism will result in the salvation of lost people. Homes will be cleansed of the filthy, trashy literature that eats away the vitals of their youth. Lives will be changed when churches get on fire for God. Every Christian should work and pray to make his a New Testament church.

The influence of the saved is needed. "Ye are the light of the world." Parents might as well let their children eat out of a garbage can and think that they will stay well as to let them read what all too many read and hope that their minds will think rightly. Oh, for a compassion among the people of our churches that will produce the right kind of living and conduct!

If Christ has his way, Christians will so live that others can see Jesus in them. When believers live Christ, lost people are convinced. When this happens, sinners are saved. What the world needs more than to hear a sermon is to see one in action. This takes place in New Testament churches when the fires of evangelistic fervor burn brightly.

2. God Glorified

When a New Testament church does its duty, God will be glorified and Christ will be magnified. The Word of God will increase greatly. The Lord will add to New Testament churches daily those who will be trusting him.

What a pity for a church to go months without professions

of faith in Christ! When Christians do God's will during the weekdays, sinners will make public profession of Christ in every service on every Lord's Day. This is possible in every church. For this to happen, pastors and church members must be willing to pay the price of consecration. Preacher and people must be willing to do God's will. They must lead the churches to utilize the organizations and methods which have upon them the evident blessing of the Lord for reaching, teaching, winning, developing, and using people.

When the price is paid, dividends are received. And "unto him be glory in the church by Christ Jesus throughout all ages, world without end. Amen" (Eph. 3:21).

QUESTIONS FOR REVIEW

1. Define a church.
2. What is the chief business of a church?
3. Name and discuss the church ordinances.
4. With what is a church equipped?
5. What does the book of the Acts of the Apostles reveal about a New Testament church?

4

Enlargement for Evangelism

> "Our mouth is open unto you, our heart is enlarged. . . .
> Be ye also enlarged" (2 Cor. 6: 11, 13).

THERE ARE several areas in which enlargement is necessary for growing bigger and better churches in order to do a bigger and better job of evangelism. In this chapter several of these areas will be discussed.

I. ENLARGED VISION IS NECESSARY

The pastor, educational director, and general superintendent must have a vision of the worth of the Sunday school in growing a church if a church is to make the most possible progress.

Isaiah saw the Lord high and lifted up; then he saw himself (Isa. 6: 1–5). This explains Isaiah's convictions; proper vision produced them. It makes a difference when people see the purity and glory of God. When the brightness of God's countenance shines in on one's soul, his whole outlook on life is changed. It takes vision such as Isaiah had to bring about a surrender that leads one to cry out, "Here am I; send me."

God took Ezekiel out into a valley that was full of dry bones and revealed to him a picture that never again let his passion for souls wane. "Where there is no vision, the people perish" (Prov. 29: 18).

1. *Vision of the Lostness of People*

Spiritual leaders must have a vision of what it means for people to be lost before they will do their best to reach men for Christ. There is no middle ground; people are either

41

saved or lost. When leaders realize this, they do something about it.

2. Vision of Salvation by Grace

Church leaders need a vision of what it means for a lost, guilty sinner to be saved.

(1) *A new life.*—John 3:16 must live in one's heart for one to understand the true meaning of the word "salvation." One may not be able in this life to understand it all, but one who experiences forgiveness for sin through faith in Jesus Christ begins to have a partial knowledge of what it means. Salvation means more than being delivered from the penalty of sin. It means being saved to eternal life with Christ and all that is involved in being present with him for eternity. Salvation means forgiveness from sin (Eph. 1:7). It means birth to a new life (John 3:3, 7).

(2) *A new relationship.*—God delivers us from the power of darkness and translates us into the kingdom of his dear Son (Col. 1:13). He causes us to sit together with Christ in heavenly places (Eph. 2:6). We are adopted into the family of God (John 1:12; Eph. 1:5). We are delivered from the curse of the law and made heirs of God and joint heirs with Jesus Christ (Rom. 8:14–17). "Ye are . . . a royal priesthood, an holy nation, a peculiar people" (1 Peter 2:9). More than that, Christ keeps us, he intercedes for us, and he will glorify us at his coming (John 10:28–29; Heb. 7:25).

(3) *A new responsibility.*—Salvation is a gift, but man must accept it. Christ died for the whole world, but the only way the whole world will know it is for born-again people to tell it to those yet lost. Before Christians do their "utmost" to carry the gospel to the "uttermost," there must be a genuine conviction of what it will mean to see those who are now dead in trespasses and in sin, reconciled unto God.

3. Vision of the Adequacy and Availability of the Sunday School

Leaders need an enlarged vision of the opportunities through the Sunday school.

(1) *The Sunday school is adequate.*—The Sunday school offers the best way known to man to reach the most people in the shortest time with the gospel. Christians are to go into all the world and preach the gospel to every creature. This is the main business of New Testament churches. A genuine conception of the real value of the Sunday school organization by the pastor and his church will make a vast difference in carrying out the commission of Jesus Christ.

Many pastors say that from 85 to 90 per cent of the people who profess faith in Christ come through the Sunday school. A functioning Sunday school program is a proved, tried, tested way to success in reaching people for Christ. Since most people are enlisted in some Sunday school class before they make their decision to follow Jesus, every effort possible should be exerted to enrol people in Bible study.

(2) *The Sunday school is available.*—The Sunday school belongs to the church; it is the church. It works at the task of reaching people for Bible study; then wins them to Christ. The Bible is the textbook of the Sunday school. The Sunday school has in it the best soul-winners. The possibilities for evangelism are in it. It is available; use it.

II. Enlarged Faith Is Necessary

"Without faith it is impossible to please him" (Heb. 11:6).

1. *Faith in Christ*

Christian leaders must have faith in Christ. They must believe that Christ is man's one and only hope. They must believe with Simon Peter: "Neither is there salvation in any other: for there is none other name under heaven given among men, whereby we must be saved" (Acts 4:12). They must believe that, even lost and ruined as man is, God offers him forgiveness, peace, and pardon through Jesus Christ.

Christian workers must have a conviction that Jesus Christ is the answer. Officers and teachers will not lead others to faith in Christ unless their own faith in him is strong.

Christ is all sufficient to meet every human need. He has proved that he is. A review of the past, by anyone who has been saved by Christ's power and kept by his grace, will help to enlarge one's faith and confidence in Jesus Christ. Those who would lead others to faith in Christ must be able to say with Paul, "I know whom I have believed, and am persuaded that he is able to keep that which I have committed unto him against that day" (2 Tim. 1:12).

2. *Faith in Others*

To be a good worker or leader in a New Testament church, one must not only have faith in Christ, one must also have faith in others. There is good in everyone if it is sought for, discovered, and brought out. We may not be able to see very much of it, but it is there. One of the major values of the Sunday school is as an enlistment agency for uncovering and developing the potential talent for service within each redeemed individual.

Often Christian workers, in trying to find others to fill places of service, look above the heads of those who are available—those who are willing, capable, yet untrained. The way to find new workers is to take the people who are available in the membership of the church, seek them out, pray for them, enlist them in training, and train them to do the task. Take people as they are and train them to be what they ought and can be. Belief in people is a prerequisite to good leadership.

God saw in Moses something that no one else had seen. Man could have seen in Moses only one who had killed an Egyptian and was hiding in the wilderness from the law of Pharaoh. God saw in him a great deliverer, a law-giver, a great leader for his people—if only Moses would surrender his life, his will, and his way to the will and wishes of Jehovah. God trusted Moses. Who but God would have entrusted to Moses what he did? God saw something in him. God believed in him.

No one but God could have seen in rugged, headstrong, impulsive Simon Peter a dynamic gospel preacher. After Peter surrendered to Jesus, he became a "rocklike" character with conviction and power. He preached at Pentecost, and three thousand souls were saved.

Look at that man, Saul of Tarsus! When one first sees him, he is a persecutor of the living Christ. The Christian leaders of that day were afraid of him. The Lord Jesus Christ saw in him one who would become, if he would yield himself to the Lord, the outstanding interpreter of the life of Christ; one who would write more than half the books of the New Testament; one who would make more missionary journeys and organize more churches than any other man of his generation. God saw something in Saul that others could not see.

God sees something in people that we cannot see. He has a purpose for every life, and that purpose should be found. As Christians we must have faith in God and faith in people. We must believe that any life, if surrendered to do so, can and will be used to the glory of Christ in the advancement of his cause. We must come to visualize what a sinner can become when Christ controls him. Confidence in others is necessary in a successful effort to enlist the necessary workers for the program of a growing, functioning Sunday school, and for other areas of the work of a church.

3. *Faith in Oneself*

One must have faith in himself. One does not often accomplish that which he does not believe that he can do. It takes faith in oneself to challenge one to try. Paul said, "As much as in me is, I am ready" (Rom. 1:15). He also said, "I can do all things through Christ which strengtheneth me" (Phil. 4:13). Strong Christian leaders can develop self-confidence in others.

A leader must not only believe that Christ is sufficient and that others can be made to become useful, but he must believe that he can be used of God to lead others to surrender to Christ. There are enough potential workers in every church to do the task that ought to be done by that church. These must be enlisted and trained to be useful.

III. ENLARGED PHYSICAL FACILITIES ARE NECESSARY

Physical equipment is absolutely essential if the best work is to be done.

1. *Land Is Essential*

Every church ought to secure plenty of property. Available property adjoining the church property should be purchased for the future need. Building requires space. The time has come when churches must have off-street parking. This is necessary to reaching people; therefore serious consideration should be given to it by every pastor.

One pastor made an appeal for six months to his people to buy the two blocks adjoining their property. Some of the people in that church had short vision; they had no idea of the amount of space that the church would need in the future. After about six months, one man who had been opposed to the enlarged program because he could not see the need of additional property came and said: "Pastor, if you would come down to earth and be reasonable in this thing, I would lead out in a program to buy one of those city blocks."

Before he could finish his conversation, the pastor had a pencil and piece of paper before him to sign a statement to that effect before he changed his mind. A city block was purchased in the next few weeks. Space holds the key. Inside and outside, churches must have plenty of property.

Too often, good businessmen see the need of enlarging their businesses, but for some reason they do not see the need of an enlarged program for God. Many of them are willing to keep pace with physical and material needs of the people of their city. On the other hand, they have not lifted up their eyes and looked on the fields that are white unto harvest. Pastors must lead them to enlarged vision.

2. *Buildings Are Necessary*

A new pastor was trying to lead his church into a building program. Someone made the statement: "Our church has gone only the distance of one man's vision." That man was not named. However, a building was necessary if more people were to be reached. A survey was made, and it showed that the buildings they had were inadequate. They were saturated. All the space was filled, and yet there were hundreds of possibilities in the city.

One day the newspaper carried a two-page spread of a certain business concern in the city whose owner was a member of that particular church. The caption on the two-page spread was: "THIS BUSINESS BELIEVES IN KEEPING PACE WITH THE NEEDS OF THE PEOPLE OF THE CITY." Underneath the caption was a picture of the present building with the back end knocked out, and workmen were erecting an addition. That skilful businessman was doubling the space of his building in order to meet the needs of the people of the city.

The pastor was not a trickster, but neither was he asleep nor blind to a truth. He felt honored to have a businessman in his church who had such far-reaching vision. He took that two-page spread, folded it up neatly, and put it into his files. He said to himself, "Old boy, you may need that someday."

A few months later, the pastor did need that spread. Plans for an additional educational unit to the church were drawn. A letter went out from the church office to all the people, stating that two weeks from that date the church would vote on a building program. All the people were urged to come and express themselves in the matter. The time came; the people were there. The building committee presented plans for the proposed educational building, then asked whether anyone had anything to say.

The man who, a few weeks before, had put the two-page spread in the paper came to the front. He said: "There are thirteen reasons why our church is not in any position to build right now, and why we should not engage in this project." He named them off one by one.

When the businessman had finished, the pastor got up and pulled that two-page spread out of his pocket. He gently unfolded it and held it before his people for a minute. They remembered it. Then he calmly said: "Dear Christian friends, your pastor is only interested in doing for the spiritual needs of the people of this city what our friend who has just spoken is interested in doing for himself, in providing for the physical and material needs of the people of this city."

After the people had visualized once again that two-page spread and had come to see the real purpose in launching a building program, they stood and voted to proceed immediately with the building program. More than that, it was not long before that particular businessman came to say: "Pastor, you put it in a different light than I had ever thought of it. I had never been conscious of the fact that, just as in the business world, we must keep expanding and enlarging in order to meet the spiritual needs of the people. I see and understand. Never again will I oppose a project that will be for the advancement of the cause of Christ."

Churches can never reach more people than they provide physical facilities to accommodate. For several months the writer has kept check on the growth of a little boy. The mother and grandmother of that child take great pride in making his clothes. But almost every time they make a new suit, they must have a new pattern or add a little on each side of the old pattern, allowing for growth.

This writer has noticed several churches that need the pattern enlarged; yet they still are using the old one. On the other hand, he has seen many churches which have kept enlarging from year to year to allow for growth, and they have grown. Churches that have not enlarged the pattern to make growth possible are no larger now than they were five, ten, fifteen, or twenty-five years ago.

A deacon visited the pastor of a church in a distant city one day. Because of years of friendship, this Christian could ask the preacher a blunt question: "Preacher, why has our church not made any progress in the last twenty-five years when churches all about us are growing in leaps and bounds?" Said he: "One church to the north of us has added space every year to take care of their fast-growing needs. To the south of us the same thing has taken place. To the west of us the church has literally tripled herself. The church on the east also has made great strides of progress. Our church has just held her own for twenty-five years. What is the reason?"

The preacher hesitated a moment and then asked: "How long has it been, Deacon, since your church added some space? How long has it been since you built some new rooms, added some new classes, some new departments, or put more workers to work?"

The deacon scratched his head and thought a moment and said, "I believe that the present building was built twenty-seven years ago."

The preacher answered: "There is your answer. You have not enlarged your building. You have not built any more space. You have not added any more classes in twenty-seven years and you have not grown any in twenty-five years. Your Sunday school has taken the shape of your building. The only way for you to grow is to add more space and enlist more workers and enlarge your organization."

A church will take the shape of the building in which it meets. The Sunday school is going to take the shape of its space. Some churches—most churches—need to add more space to their present buildings. Most Baptist churches have new buildings filled by the time they are ready to enter. This is a healthy situation. However, as long as this is the case, a church should keep on enlarging and providing space. It will be filled, other things being equal.

Most Baptist churches can reach as many people as they are willing to provide space to care for. To grow a great Sunday school is to grow a great church. This can be done only when proper space is provided and an adequate organization is set up for the task.

The laws of growth apply to all the units and all the organization of a New Testament church. They hold true in the Training Union, Woman's Missionary Union, Brotherhood, and any other agency of the church. We put more people to work, provide more space; then we reach more people. Therefore make preparation now to enlarge the organizations, to move up from what you now have to the next step in the pattern of growth.

IV. ENLARGED ORGANIZATION IS NECESSARY

The laws of Sunday school growth are as exacting as the law of gravity.

1. *Observe the Ten-to-One Law of Growth*

Southern Baptists have found over a period of years that a church can reach a maximum of about ten people for every worker who is enlisted and trained. Then the organization saturates; the growth becomes static.

The writer decided that he would test this thing out for himself. The first church he checked had 601 in Sunday school with 60 workers. The second church had 787 in Sunday school and they had 78 workers. The third in the test revealed 1,178 in Sunday school with 117 workers. One had 2,200 in Sunday school with 220 workers, and another 70 with 7. In each case the pastor of the church was asked to count the workers. These were churches using the same pattern for the past several years—no new classes and departments had been started in months.

A Sunday school saturates when it reaches the ten-to-one ratio. It ceases to reach additional people. Therefore, if a church wants to reach ten additional people, it is essential to enlist and train at least one more teacher. If a church desires to reach a hundred additional people, it is just as simple as enlisting and training ten additional workers and giving them places to meet, with lists of prospects. To reach more people, more workers must be put to work.

2. *Observe the Law Relating to New Units*

The number of units should be increased. New units reach people faster than old ones. Every Sunday school should be on a constant lookout for an opportunity to add new departments or classes or both.

3. *Step Up the Organization*

There are thousands of class schools that should move up to departments immediately. It has been proved that this is the best way to grow bigger and better Sunday schools. If your church is a class school, you are limited in your outreach for people. As soon as possible, build space to take care of a department organization. Perhaps the space you now have could be rearranged for departments. Start as many new classes as you can. A church will not enlarge beyond the vision of its leaders, nor will it attempt more than their faith prompts. Noninterested, unenlisted people will not demand that a church prepare a place for them. They are not that concerned. They are not expected to be.

It is the God-given and the Holy Spirit-empowered task of New Testament churches to see to it that the pattern and organization be kept adequate to meet the needs of the people to be reached. The organization must be enlarged. Not all of the people in a church can readily see this, but someone must have a vision of the needs. Faith must accompany this vision, or the necessary steps for enlarging the pattern and organization will not be taken.

Some churches need to move up from the class pattern to the department pattern for the Sunday school. Space holds the key, but space can be provided. Many class schools could take the first step up even in their present buildings, without additional space. If a room is large enough for the Beginners or the Primaries to use during the class period, then usually a department for that age group could meet in it during the whole Sunday school hour.

Class Sunday schools have served their day well, but the day has come when practically every class school could and should become a department school. A class school can reach only so many people and no more. To move up to a department pattern would mean that more people would be reached.

Many churches with one department for each age span ought to move up to two departments for each age span.

Those churches that now have two should be looking forward to the time when they can have multiple departments.

4. *Rearrange Space*

One church was reminded that with just a little excavating a ground-level floor could be made under the present church building, thus doubling its capacity. This was done. Another church took some big rooms that were in the educational building and made them into assembly rooms with adjoining classrooms. Instead of one class wasting all that space, now a department with several classes uses the same space.

Everything possible should be done to use the space that is available to the best advantage for the whole program of the church. In many cases additional classrooms can be made by dividing some of the larger rooms. Many churches have made rooms in hallways or in storage rooms. Often a department can be divided and two departments can use the space formerly used by one.

In a certain church there was a huge room up by the tower that had no entrance. It was of no value. A wise leader had a stairway erected up to the room and so made it possible to start a second Primary department.

A certain church was convinced that every available space was occupied. No one thought any more in terms of new classes and departments. The new pastor who came on the field did not know about all that. He studied the situation himself. He had a committee to come and study it with him. They started shifting and rearranging classes and departments and were able to add thirteen classes to that Sunday school. In five months the net gain, as a result of that, was 125. Rearrange your space; make the best possible use of all your floor space.

It was the custom of the writer during his pastorate to lead his church to adopt a policy in regard to the space in the church. It was church property. No teacher or superintendent had a lease on any room or rooms. At any time during the year that it became necessary to shift any department, class, or classes, in order to rearrange the space to provide for more people, the church had voted to do so. The workers were all committed to this policy by the church when they were elected. This relieved many problems. It gave opportunity to put growing classes in space that was not being used to the best advantage. It made it possible at times to start new departments which otherwise could not have been started.

I remember on one occasion we had some "morning glories" in one church. They attended only the Sunday morning worship services and yet they thought that God was highly honored by their presence. They felt that they had been a blessing to the church and to the Lord by their brief presence. The church wanted to build an educational building, but they could not see the need of additional space.

One Saturday night the pastor, the superintendent, and the educational director went into the beautiful and spacious auditorium where the people would come to worship the next morning. We stretched wires and hung curtains and made places for seven classes. The next morning those classes tried to study the Bible there. It was not a good situation, but it led to one.

The eleven o'clock hour came, and those "morning glories" entered. They saw the curtains that marred the beauty of that beautiful house of worship. One can imagine what happened. After they had their say—and it would not do to print some of their sayings—it was made plain to them that it was necessary to have classes in the places of worship in order to accommodate the people who were coming to our Sunday school.

"Oh, has it come to that?" asked one. "If it is necessary to mess up our beautiful auditorium to take care of the people we are reaching, we had better get into a building program soon," he said.

We do not necessarily recommend that procedure, but we do say, "When space is needed, provide it." Since space holds the key to growth, and since reaching people is possible only when space is provided, we are highly concerned that all churches provide all the space possible.

5. Organize New Work

New Sunday schools reach people faster than older ones. Almost every church in the Southern Baptist Convention could and should start one or more new Sunday schools. New Sunday schools average a net gain in enrolment of about sixty-five for the first year, while the best average net gain any one year for Southern Baptist churches over a year old is fourteen. One Sunday school enrolled 800 net gain in a period of a few months. Six hundred and seven of the 800 came through six arms that were extended from the church. New schools multiply the ministry of a church.

The Southern Baptist program of advance calls for more churches, more Sunday schools, more departments, and more workers.

V. ENLARGED ENROLMENT IS NECESSARY

If your Sunday school is to have a larger attendance on Sunday morning, then more people must be enrolled. On an average, 62 per cent of the enrolment of a Sunday school attend on Sunday morning. Therefore the sure way to "up" the attendance is to increase the enrolment. There are several sources from which Sunday schools can find prospects for enrolment in Bible study.

1. Church Members

A vast number of church members are not in Sunday school. This is the place to begin for an increase in enrolment. There are over two million Southern Baptists who do not live where their church membership is. They are detached. They are nonresident. One can be assured that they are not in Bible study anywhere. They should be enlisted. Then, there are practically as many resident church members in our Convention who are not enrolled in regular Bible study in any Sunday school.

There is plenty of room for enlargement in most Sunday schools from within the unenlisted church membership. Very few churches have enough space provided even for those who belong to the church. Someone should get the church roll and check it against the Sunday school roll and make a prospect card for every member of the church not enrolled in Sunday school. These prospects should be assigned to the proper departments and classes for enlistment. Either in the Extension department or in a class at the church, every member of every church should be enlisted in Bible study.

2. A Religious Census

Enlarge your Sunday school enrolment by use of a religious census. A census will provide unlimited numbers of unreached people, both lost and otherwise. Not many of the 2,000,000 "lost, strayed, or stolen" members of Southern Baptist churches are in Sunday school. Many of them would move their church membership if they could be found and then enlisted in Bible study. These Baptists could be located by our Sunday schools through a religious census. There are more than 40,000,000 unenlisted people for whom Southern Baptist Sunday schools are definitely responsible. To reach these for Bible study and for Christ is the main business of the Sunday school.

3. Visitors

The Sunday school enrolment can be enlarged by enlisting visitors who attend the worship services. A visitor's card should be given to every visitor who attends a service of the church, with the request that he fill in the blanks. Some of the best Sunday school prospects are found in this way.

4. Unenrolled Members of Families

Get enlisted members of your Sunday school to give the names of unenlisted friends and members of their families. Every Sunday school should strive to enrol every member of every family. To do this, the church must provide a place in the Sunday school for every member of every family.

Churches that major on enlisting every member of every family find it necessary to have a balanced program of work. This leads to success in reaching people. Sunday school leaders should never be satisfied until a definite effort has been made to enlist every member of every family.

Israel limited God. Jesus could do no mighty works in Nazareth because of the unbelief of the people. Make the decision right now that you, for one, will give God a chance to use you to help enlist every available person in your Sunday school for Bible study.

The decision to enlarge the pattern should be made by many. Space must be made available. Workers in sufficient number to reach all the people who ought to be reached must be trained. We should do everything in our power to enlist as many people as possible for Bible study, for Christ, and for service.

5. *Vacation Bible School*

Literally hundreds of people could and should be enlisted in Sunday school immediately after Vacation Bible school every summer. They were located as a result of the Bible school. Hundreds of boys and girls attend Vacation Bible school each summer who do not go to Sunday school. These children have parents and other members of their families who are not in Sunday school. Many of them could be enlisted in Sunday school the next Sunday. What a field for growth!

QUESTIONS FOR REVIEW

1. Name five areas for enlargement.

2. Why is vision of need so necessary?

3. What is the law relating to new units?

4. How could many Sunday schools put to better use their present space?

5

Enlisting and Training Workers
for Evangelism

"Then saith he unto his disciples, The harvest truly is plenteous, but the labourers are few; pray ye therefore the Lord of the harvest, that he will send forth labourers into his harvest" (Matt. 9:37–38).

"Study to shew thyself approved unto God, a workman that needeth not to be ashamed, rightly dividing the word of truth" (2 Tim. 2:15).

Does your church have all the Sunday school workers it needs? It could have. Are the workers in your church well trained for the task assigned them? They should and could be.

One of the essentials to a successful church program is well-trained workers. Oil and insurance companies spend literally thousands of dollars annually training their personnel. It pays good dividends or they would not do it. The average church selects Sunday school workers who have had little or no experience or training and expects them to do the job without any consideration of training them for their task. Churches cannot afford to continue doing that. The Baptist Sunday School Board, Nashville, Tennessee, has a well-planned program of training which will meet the needs of all churches that will make it available to their workers.

Why do big business concerns realize the importance of training their personnel, while leaders in churches do not see its value? Jesus said, "The children of this world are in their generation wiser than the children of light" (Luke 16:8). Could that be the answer? Churches must have leaders; leaders must be trained; therefore training opportunities must be provided.

The spiritual condition of a lost world moved Jesus to compassion. Christians today who look at the world through the eyes of Christ are also moved with compassion. The world is the field. Preaching the gospel to every creature is the task of every church. The field is white already unto harvest; yet the laborers are few. Wise leadership will be constantly on the search for new workers and will seek to enlist and train them as fast as possible.

I. EVANGELISM REQUIRES WORKERS

A survey of any community would reveal far more possibilities to be reached than most people would suppose. The multitudes are within reach and churches are responsible for them. Too few churches have enough workers enlisted to do the task. Many of those enlisted are untrained.

If the multitudes for whom Christ died are reached, they must be located. Churches must find the people before they can minister to their needs. This requires additional Sunday school workers. More departments and classes reach more people and, of course, require more workers. For every new class needed, a teacher must be enlisted and trained. Thousands of new departments and classes could and should be started in Southern Baptist Sunday schools in the near future.

Workers for all phases of church work should be carefully selected. The Sunday school is no exception. There should be certain requisites for Sunday school workers in every department.

1. *Born from Above*

The experience of the new birth is the first essential for workers in evangelism. "That which is born of the flesh is flesh; and that which is born of the Spirit is spirit" (John 3:6).

2. *Consecrated*

A pastor should never find it necessary to apologize for the conduct of his officers and teachers. They should live above reproach. Workers should grow and develop their Christian character while they attempt to help others grow in Christian graces.

3. *Willing to Learn*

Workers should be chosen of God and set apart for definite service. Christian workers should accept Christ's standard of true greatness. Jesus said, "The Son of man came not to be ministered unto, but to minister" (Matt. 20:28).

Sunday school officers and teachers must be willing to be led of the Holy Spirit into fields of service. They must serve because of their need of and devotion to Christ. They should stand willing and ready to study in order to be "approved unto God, a workman that needeth not to be ashamed, rightly dividing the word of truth" (2 Tim. 2:15).

God has not made a place of service without having someone to fill it. Too often, workers are not willing to qualify. Churches are responsible for everything necessary to enlist, train, and develop people for Christian service.

4. *Compassionate*

Lost people moved Jesus to compassion. Paul was a compassionate worker. "Therefore watch, and remember, that by the space of three years I ceased not to warn every one night and day with tears" (Acts 20:31). In Paul's writings it was compassion; in his service it was tears. To realize the real value of a soul and the length of eternity will put compassion into one's heart.

5. *Voluntary*

Only workers with the volunteer spirit can be used in God's program. No coercion or force is used to get people to serve God in the Sunday school. When sought out for service, they must be willing. Such workers are willing to train and to spend hard hours of preparation and study of the Word of God in order to be able to divide rightly his truth on the Lord's Day. They are willing to visit absentees, prospects, the sick, and the needy during the week. Volunteers, when trained for a specific task, will locate, enlist, teach, and win to Christ those who are lost, once they are given that responsibility.

Sunday school workers must have the vision of Christ for the multitudes before they are willing to give their best in service. They must realize the lostness of people. They must visualize the awfulness of the hell to which people without Christ must go, or they will never say, "Here am I; send me."

Many Christians, just as willing and ready as those now enlisted, wait for someone to enlist and train them. To angels, Jesus did not give this opportunity, but to his disciples he said, "Go ye." What a glorious privilege to join heart and hand with a volunteer band of loyal, devoted, consecrated workers in a worldwide undertaking as co-laborers with Christ in the greatest project known to man! Any day churches really try, enough capable, willing, yet untrained, potential Sunday school workers can be enlisted.

The work of volunteer workers cannot be paid for in dollars and cents. It is impossible to evaluate the time they give to their task once they are enlisted and trained. Their hours cannot be numbered. They seek not financial remuneration for their services. They have been redeemed, not with silver and gold, but with the precious blood of Jesus Christ, and in his name and for his sake are they willing to serve. Does your church have all the workers it needs?

Potential workers wait to be enlisted. Every church has enough idle people at least to double its working Sunday school force any day it takes this matter seriously. A vast majority of the workers in Southern Baptist churches are volunteers. Only eternity will reveal the full fruits of the labors of this untiring host. The urgent need is to increase the number of these volunteer workers.

II. WORKERS MUST BE ENLISTED

Jesus said: "Say not ye, There are yet four months, and then cometh harvest? behold, I say unto you, Lift up your eyes, and look on the fields; for they are white already to harvest" (John 4:35).

Ours is a tremendous task! With all the work that has been done, there is still a great need for more workers. Our task will not be completed on earth until Jesus comes. One need but lift up his eyes and look on the fields to see that they are white unto harvest. We must increase the number of workers if we are to reach the greatest number of people in the shortest time.

Our world is in an alarming condition—sin-sick, pleasure-mad, and power-crazy. We have the solution—Christ is the answer. Christ commands us to preach, teach, and win the lost. We are to begin in Jerusalem and go into all the world telling the good news. He is depending on his followers and no others to evangelize this world. There is a place of service for everyone. The right person for the right place must be enlisted. A few suggestions for enlisting workers are listed.

1. *Pray for Workers*

Jesus himself said, "Pray ye therefore the Lord of the harvest, that he will send forth labourers into his harvest" (Matt. 9:38). Workers are to pray for more workers. Laborers can be enlisted in answer to "the effectual fervent prayer of a righteous man" (James 5:16).

2. *Search for Workers*

Much searching needs to be done in order to locate the potential workers that are in every church. Leaders need to get the church roll down and study it with the view to selecting potential workers, enlisting them in training, and getting them ready for service for the Master. There is no shortage of potential laborers, but the kind some people look for are scarce. Leaders who are willing to train people for service can find all they need.

3. Call Upon Adult Sunday School Teachers for Help

Wise and happy is the teacher whose one desire is to win and develop others for service. Good, right-spirited Adult teachers can send out a constant stream of workers. One Adult teacher can produce several other workers in a year's time.

4. Preach for Workers

A plea from the pastor as he stands in the pulpit will bring results. People will surrender their lives in service to and for Christ in response to a warm, heartfelt appeal from the pastor. The preachers, better than anyone else, can be used of God to call out the called.

III. WORKERS MUST BE TRAINED

Offer ample training opportunities and workers will enlist in them. Many who are willing to serve have not been trained. When enough opportunities for training are offered, people will respond. Churches that offer adequate training opportunities to equip new workers will find that they are available and ready to serve.

Offering a few opportunities in training will not get the job done. People are too busy to take every course that is offered; therefore the answer is more courses. Not everyone will take every course, but if enough courses are offered, enough people will get in on some.

To reach the multitudes, and to reach them faster, will require many additional Sunday school workers. Trained workers make better and happier workers. Churches should provide training for them.

This is a day of specialization. Successful people are those who have specialized in a particular phase of work. Workers will major in certain fields when given an opportunity to do so. Many people hesitate to take a place of responsibility in service because they are unprepared. The right kind of training program is the answer.

The Training Union aims to train all Christians in church membership, and is adequate to do that which it sets out to do for every member who will avail himself of the opportunity. There is a great need, however, in every church for specialized workers. Opportunities for specific training should be made available for those whom God would have fill special places of service in the various fields of activity of a church. The Sunday School Training Course provides this opportunity for Sunday school workers.

How much specialized training should a church offer for Sunday school workers? The desired results, the kind of organization to be set up, the kind of teaching desired, and the efficiency expected of the workers should determine the amount and kind of training done. The amount and kind of training a church offers will determine the success of the work done. If more workers are needed, then the right kind of training program is the answer.

There are millions of undiscovered teachers and officers on the rolls of Southern Baptist churches. There is unlimited power going to waste because no one has harnessed it. Too many people have not been enlisted or trained for service.

1. *Elect a Superintendent of Training*

The superintendent of training should be an associate in the Sunday school and should be elected by the church. A church will not go beyond the vision and leadership of its pastor. Before a church will be able to have an adequate training program, the pastor, educational director (if there is one), and Sunday school superintendent must be sold on it. They, in turn, must work with the superintendent of training in order to have a program that will meet the needs of the Sunday school.

There are potential workers sufficient to set up the Sunday school organization necessary to reach and minister to all the people that ought to be reached in any given community.

But many of these potential workers are standing by idle. They are ready; they are willing; they are just as capable as those now serving; yet they have not been enlisted and trained. It is the task of the leaders of a church to realize this fact and to work out a program of training that will achieve the greatest results. Unless someone is made responsible for this particular phase of church life, it will continue to be neglected.

2. Plan a Program

A program of training for Sunday school workers should be planned each year well in advance. Serious consideration should be given to the question, "How much training?" The amount of training needed will depend on the achievements desired. Decide what your church should do and train for it.

Each church, of course, will correlate its training in the Calendar of Activities for the year to meet the needs of the whole program. The church calendar should offer courses selected from each of the departments of the church—the Sunday school, Training Union, Woman's Missionary Union, Brotherhood—courses for deacons, courses on missions. A special week of emphasis on music and other phases of the church life should be included in the calendar of training. The associate superintendent of the Sunday school in charge of training will be responsible mainly for getting the courses pertaining to Sunday school work included in the church calendar.

Methods and administration books should be included. There should be a week included in the Calendar of Activities of every church as early in October each year as possible to train new workers in the fields of service for which the church has made them responsible.

Some pastors use part of every Wednesday night to teach some Bible book to the membership. This offers the people a marvelous opportunity in systematic Bible study. Studies such as this will enrich the pastor's life and also the lives of those who attend. Where this has been done constantly and properly, the attendance in prayer meeting has increased.

A "loafers' class" has been helpful in some churches. There are many people who wait around the church for other members of the family who are in the officers and teachers' meeting. These people would be glad to be in a training course rather than waste their time. Start a class for them. Name it "Loafers Class." They will like it. Such books as *Baptist Distinctives, These Things We Believe, Our Doctrines,* or some other book on doctrine would be a blessing to them. Many officers and teachers have come out of such classes.

As a pastor, I felt responsible to include every year, in the Calendar of Activities, four of the basic diploma books for Sunday school workers as suggested by the Sunday School Department of the Baptist Sunday School Board. If challenged to do so, people will take these four books during the year, looking forward to commencement, at which time the church will award the diplomas in recognition of advancement in training. Every new worker in the Sunday school should have opportunity during his first year of service to take the four basic books required to receive the Worker's Diploma.

Churches should correlate the training program. There are certain books offered with interchangeable credit. All courses should be planned in advance and placed in the Calendar of Activities before it is presented to the church each year for adoption. Then the training program becomes a church program. Department books should be offered every year so that the workers of the departments can know their specific duties.

Group and individual studies should be encouraged and accepted as a part of the training program. Emphasis should be given to state and Convention-wide assemblies as training opportunities. Only eternity will reveal the real worth of Ridgecrest and Glorieta to our program of training.

3. *Adopt the Training Program*

The program should be adopted by the church. Anything as important to a church as a well-balanced program of training should have the support of that church. The church budget should include in it the expenses of the training program. There will be books to buy, equipment to purchase. The expenses of the annual banquet and commencement should also be provided by the church.

4. *Promote the Training Program*

Use every means available to keep the program before the church.

(1) *Publicize the program.*—From the pulpit, through the church bulletin, the newspapers, the radio, the bulletin boards, posters, and any other conceivable way, see to it that the people are informed as to the time when training opportunities will be offered. Training dates should be kept everlastingly before the people. All coming events should be publicized regularly.

(2) *Hold an annual training banquet.*—A good way to stimulate interest in a training program is to plan an annual training banquet for all of the workers who have trained during the year.

(3) *Hold an annual commencement.*—Commencement exercises which recognize certain achievements in the training program for Sunday school workers have been a blessing to many churches. Do not be afraid to keep the training emphasis constantly before the church. Even the best-trained and educated people get enthusiastic over the commencement exercises.

(4) *Display the diplomas.*—Display all of the diplomas in the hallways, secondary auditorium, or educational building of the church. Neatly arranged on the wall, they inspire others to train for service.

(5) *Stay everlastingly at it.*—It is not enough to realize the need in the matter of training, nor will presenting a well-outlined program to the church be sufficient. A program of this type requires weeks and months of hard work. It is never finished, but if carried on properly, it will produce everlasting results. Plenty of workers will always be available. The church that offers adequate opportunities for training will always have workers ready when needed.

In the spring of 1947, the Toulminville Baptist Church, Mobile, Alabama, broke ground for an educational unit to provide for an additional one thousand in Sunday school. The organization would need to be doubled at the time the new unit was entered.

The Sunday school had never been fully graded. The people had to be taught the proper appreciation for, and the absolute necessity of, a fully graded school to get the full benefit of the new building and to reach the possibilities that were there.

Up to that time the church had never had a weekly officers and teachers' meeting. It was evident that an adequate training program would help get the value of such a meeting over to our people.

A careful checkup on the workers of the school revealed that only a few had even the Worker's Diploma. The real need was a training program to train those then working, and to train prospective teachers and officers for the enlarged program that was ahead. The church had had study courses at convenient seasons but without definite purpose, and too many times no record was kept nor was the course reported to the Sunday School Board for awards or records.

The pastor and a few other leaders had been to one of the Sunday School Weeks at Ridgecrest that year. The training program of the Sunday School Department of the Sunday School Board had been most effectively presented. The pastor and superintendent took the suggestions made there and started out to do something that had never been attempted in that church.

A superintendent of training, an associate in the Sunday school, was enlisted and elected by the church to be responsible for, and in charge of, the program for the year. A program of Sunday school training was worked out as part of the church Calendar of Activities, and was adopted by the church.

The basic Worker's Diploma books were included in the program. The pastor agreed to teach the Bible books in the midweek prayer services. This took about three months for each book. Other classes were arranged at every available time when a few of the teachers and officers could meet. A goal of sixty Worker's Diplomas was set for the year.

To create interest and to challenge the people to faithfulness in the training program, plans were made for the annual Sunday school worker's banquet which was had in December of that year. The plan for a graduation service for Sunday school workers was adopted. It has come to be called "Annual Workers' Commencement." The state Sunday school secretary, E. A. Herron, was enlisted to bring the message.

The program was outlined in detail and presented to the church for adoption. The church got behind it. It really "went over." The spirit for training ran high. The church voted to pay the expenses of the program, including books, equipment, materials, and the expenses of the banquet and commencement.

The attendance was good, increasing in each successive class for one of the diploma books. The banquet and the commencement were kept before the church. Interest soared higher throughout the period. Additional classes at various times were conducted. When the people got interested in training, they were hard to satisfy. Workers began working on extra books at home.

When the program for the first year was completed, sixty-six received the Worker's Diploma. During the period the average attendance of Sunday school almost doubled; the workers were the happiest that they had ever been. The entire church took on new life.

When the new building was entered, it was no trouble to enlarge the organization to twice its size. Workers were ready. The pastor had taught most of the books and he taught with a purpose. It was easy to grade the school fully, for the people had been trained for it and the building had been planned with a fully graded Sunday school in mind. The workers had come to see the need for, and the value of, the weekly officers and teachers' meetings also. From then until now the Sunday school has regularly had most effective weekly meetings. That school has continued upward all these years. It has doubled its size several times. The church still feels the effect of that training.

In that first commencement a man fifty-five years of age received his diploma. When the pastor, assisted by the superintendent of training, awarded the diploma he shouted out: "I never graduated anywhere in my life before." He was "thrilled to death."

Three men who had watched the people receive their diplomas came up to the pastor at the close of the service and one of them, acting as spokesman, said, "Pastor, what did Mr. X do to wear that cap and gown and get that diploma?"

The pastor said: "He took the course. For four full weeks, five nights a week, Mr. X attended the courses here at the church."

The three chimed in and said, "Pastor, when are you going to start the next course?"

In other words, at least three prospects, who had never thought of it before, were waiting to get in the next course offered in training. In fact, literally dozens of people felt as those three men did, and from that day it was no trouble to enlist potential workers in the training program.

The training program was so much help and created such fine spirit in the church that it was adopted as an annual affair. Instead of finding a half-dozen Worker's Diplomas when one enters the vestibule of the educational building in that church, one sees, beautifully displayed in uniform frames, dozens of Worker's Diplomas, Advanced Diplomas, and Master Diplomas, with any number of Red, Blue, and Gold Seals attached.

When the people are challenged, a church can have workers to do all the jobs that need to be done. Training should be brought to the front in our churches. No longer should it be kept in the background. Magnify and dignify it and people will receive it.

IV. TRAINING INCREASES EVANGELISM

Through personal witnessing of trained soul-winners, the lost are brought to a saving knowledge of Christ. Through teaching done by trained workers, saints are edified. They grow in grace and knowledge and go out as new recruits in service for Christ. Through their contacts individuals are made stronger in faith.

The one who does his best for Christ has the satisfaction of being well pleasing to God. This brings peace that passeth all understanding to the human heart. The trained volunteer worker looks forward to the time when he will hear the Heavenly Father say, "Well done, thou good and faithful servant: thou hast been faithful over a few things, I will make thee ruler over many things: enter thou into the joy of thy lord" (Matt. 25:21).

If your Sunday school needs grading, then train for it. If you need a new building, train your people and you will get it. If you need more workers, then the right kind of training program is the answer. If you want better teaching, then train your teachers. If you need new departments or classes, then use your training program to prepare your people for them. If your church needs the spirit of evangelism, then train for it. If your church needs the spirit of missions that will cause you to break bounds and go into other areas and start new Sunday schools, then train your people to do it. Training is a big job, but it is well worth everything that it takes.

QUESTIONS FOR REVIEW

1. State the law of Sunday school growth relating to workers.

2. Where are workers to be found?

3. How are workers to be found and enlisted?

4. Outline a church training program.

5. Give some suggestions for promoting the training program in a church.

6

Perennial Evangelism

"And they, continuing daily with one accord in the temple, . . . the Lord added to the church daily" (Acts 2:46–47).

"And daily in the temple, and in every house, they ceased not to teach and preach Jesus Christ" (Acts 5:42).

"And the things that thou hast heard of me among many witnesses, the same commit thou to faithful men, who shall be able to teach others also" (2 Tim. 2:2).

JESUS CHRIST is depending on his churches to be instrumental in preaching the gospel to every creature. Churches are to use every means available to get the message of the Bible to the people.

I. THE NEW TESTAMENT TYPE OF EVANGELISM IS THE WORK OF A CHURCH

It is tremendously important that followers of Christ understand clearly what they are commissioned to do while here on earth. New Testament churches not only have the message, they have the mission. Christ himself is the message, and he assigned the mission. Churches know how to reach people with the message of redemption. They know the best-tried, successful methods of reaching people with the message. The school of the church is adequate for this task. The work of evangelism has no parallel. Nothing can take its place. A church cannot neglect it and prosper.

II. NEW TESTAMENT EVANGELISM IS PERENNIAL

"All at it all the time" is, perhaps, a good way to state it. Special efforts for evangelism are most fruitful. Churches should never abandon the plan of having special quests for souls. At least twice each year an intensified effort in evangelism should be put forth by every church. Failure to do so cannot be excused. However, this is only a part of the work of evangelism.

Perennial evangelism makes special quests even more effective. Churches that constantly labor at the task, week after week, can usually be more successful in major seasonal opportunities. Churches that continually use tested, successful Sunday school methods for reaching people can see visible results every week in the year, and when special efforts are put forth, the harvest will be even greater.

III. THE SUNDAY SCHOOL IS THE CHURCH AT WORK IN YEAR-ROUND EVANGELISM

The Word says: "Be instant in season, out of season" (2 Tim. 4:2). Christ means for his churches to be going and making disciples, and baptizing and teaching to observe.

The Sunday school is the school of the church. There was a time when Sunday schools were not operated by the church. In our day New Testament churches have come to realize the value and importance of using the Sunday school in carrying out the program of evangelism.

1. Officers and Teachers Are Elected by the Church

The church elects the officers and teachers of its Sunday school. The school is responsible to make monthly or quarterly reports to the church. All Sunday school work is church work.

2. The Sunday School Is Financed by the Church

In all cases the church should finance the cost of operating its Sunday school.

3. The Sunday School Is the Church

Churches have found that the Sunday school is the best medium through which the Bible can be taught regularly and systematically to more people. Some phases of New Testament evangelism can best be done through the use of the Sunday school.

Churches have found the Sunday school to be the greatest soul-winning agency available. The Sunday school is the church. It is the church enlisting people for Bible study. It is the church teaching the Bible to the masses. It is the church questing for souls and winning the lost to Christ and utilizing them in Christian service.

Perennial evangelism is the major work of a church. Many and varied are the activities of a wide-awake church. However, there are things that should be given major emphasis. Far too many major on minors.

IV. A Functioning Sunday School Ensures Perennial Soul-Winning

Making disciples is a continuous job. It must be a major emphasis of a church. A church is equipped with its Sunday school to make disciples, not just occasionally, but every week in the year.

1. *The Sunday School Has the Message That Makes Disciples*

Evangelism is the proclamation of the gospel for the salvation of the soul and the life of the individual. Bible evangelism starts with the individual where he is—lost and ruined because of sin—and follows through until he comes "unto the measure of the stature of the fulness of Christ" (Eph. 4:13).

The gospel is the good news that God, through Jesus Christ, will reconcile unto himself any and all who will accept his salvation. John the Baptist expressed it thus: "Behold the Lamb of God, which taketh away the sin of the world" (John 1:29). Simon Peter, one who learned the good news firsthand, said, "Neither is there salvation in any other: for there is none other name under heaven given among men, whereby we must be saved" (Acts 4:12). Paul, called to be an apostle, said, "This is a faithful saying, and worthy of all acceptation, that Christ Jesus came into the world to save sinners; of whom I am chief" (1 Tim. 1 : 15).

Jesus summed up the gospel in these words: "For God so loved the world, that he gave his only begotten Son, that whosoever believeth in him should not perish, but have everlasting life" (John 3 : 16).

The secret of the marvelous success of Southern Baptist churches lies in the emphasis which they place on evangelism. Many things are important; evangelism is primal. Churches that have recognized and taken advantage of the opportunities for evangelism through the Sunday school have been most successful in carrying out the Great Commission of their Lord.

If a church fails to evangelize the local community, there is no one else to do it. A church has no better way than through its Sunday school to proclaim the gospel to all the people to whom it is responsible.

2. *The Sunday School Has the Messengers*

Next perhaps in importance to the evangel is the evangelist. The evangel is the good news that God will save people from their sins; an evangelist is one who proclaims that good news to those in sin. Every Christian is to be an evangelist.

When Christ instituted his church, he endowed it with power and equipped it for teaching the Word of God. He, himself, was the master Teacher of all times. He keeps alive his teaching in the world today through that vast host of Sunday school teachers who give themselves, from Sunday to Sunday, to telling the "good news."

3. *The Sunday School Has in It the Potentials for Disciples*

For teachers or evangelists to proclaim with success the gospel, there must be someone to hear and receive it. The most adequate and effective means that we have today to enlist people in the study of the gospel is the Sunday school.

When the Sunday school is recognized and used for that purpose, victory is certain.

Churches win to Christ each year one out of every three lost people enlisted in Bible study; whereas, of that vast multitude of lost people not enlisted in Sunday school, only one out of 240 is won to Christ each year. To consider seriously this matter would drive churches to a more intensive and successful use of the Sunday school.

4. *The Sunday School Marches Under Divine Orders*

Making disciples is not optional with a church or its school; it is imperative. Jesus said, "Make disciples of all nations." He also said, "Ye shall be witnesses unto me both in Jerusalem, and in all Judaea, and in Samaria, and unto the uttermost part of the earth" (Acts 1:8). Again he said, "Behold, I send you forth" (Matt. 10:16). He also said, "As my Father hath sent me, even so send I you" (John 20:21).

Making disciples involves several things: locating the prospects, enlarging the organization, providing adequate space, and enlisting and training workers. A visitation program is absolutely essential if a church is to get the best results in "discipling" people through the Sunday school.

5. *The Sunday School Is Organized to Make Disciples*

The Bible-teaching program of a church is channeled through the Sunday school. The Sunday school provides regular Bible study for all the people—saved and unsaved. Sunday school officers and teachers are trained and given places of responsibility with the purpose of making disciples. The units are kept small so that the best possible work may be done to this end. The constituency is graded into small groups by ages, where personal attention is given.

6. *The Sunday School Meets at the Right Time to Make Disciples*

The Sunday school meets immediately before the preaching hour. It puts the people into the worship service, where decisions are called for. The warm atmosphere of a worship service immediately following a period of Bible study is conducive to surrender to Christ, thus leading people to become his followers.

V. "Teaching Them" Becomes Perennial Through the Sunday School

Teaching his Word is one of the grandest privileges and yet one of the gravest responsibilities that God has given to his church. The Great Commission includes, "Teaching them to observe all things whatsoever I have commanded you" (Matt. 28 : 20). In season and out of season this is to go on—there must be no letup—all at it, all the time. This is perennial evangelism; and the Sunday school does it.

Jesus spent much of his earthly ministry teaching. Again and again, the Bible refers to Jesus as "teacher" or "teaching." New Testament evangelism requires much teaching. People must be taught. Information is necessary to proper response and development. Churches must teach. The Sunday school has something to teach; and it is at its best when teaching.

1. *The Sunday School Is Equipped to Teach the Bible*

More people study the Bible in Sunday school than in any other way. In fact, people who are not in Sunday school do not do much Bible study.

(1) *The Bible is the textbook of the Sunday school.*—It is the central thing on Sunday morning. The teacher who thoroughly prepares his lesson before time to teach can use his Bible in the class to the advantage of each individual pupil.

The Bible has a message in it for every child of God, every born-again believer in Christ, as well as for the lost. Teachers who faithfully teach the message of the Book prove a blessing to those in the class.

All too many people who have come to know Jesus in the forgiveness of sin have not realized the value of his Word. It is the duty of a New Testament church, not only to win a person to Christ, but to teach him the Word of God. "All scripture is given by inspiration of God, and is profitable for doctrine, for reproof, for correction, for instruction in righteousness" (2 Tim. 3:16). "For the prophecy came not in old time by the will of man: but holy men of God spake as they were moved by the Holy Ghost" (2 Peter 1:21).

Churches that utilize their Sunday school teachers to magnify the Bible every Sunday and throughout every week in the year will be successful. People who are won to Christ and the church will be edified and built up in the faith by a Bible-centered ministry.

(2) *The Bible is the standard of faith and conduct for the Christian.*—A New Testament church must hold high the standard for Christian living. The Bible is the chart and compass for the Christian. A good teacher will help to make the Bible a lamp and a light for the feet and a pathway of those in his class. The Bible provides guideposts for those who would advance in the direction of God's standard of righteousness. Sunday school teachers, better than anyone else, can help people find the way to God's will for their lives.

(3) *The Bible serves as a fire, a sword, and a hammer for a teacher.*—"Is not my word like as a fire? saith the Lord; and like a hammer that breaketh the rock in pieces?" (Jer. 23:29). "For the word of God is quick, and powerful, and sharper than any twoedged sword, piercing even to the dividing asunder of soul and spirit, and of the joints and marrow, and is a discerner of the thoughts and intents of the heart" (Heb. 4:12). Teachers, use it! Believe in its power. Victory will be certain.

There are many things that people should know, but the greatest knowledge is for one to know God. It is for one's own benefit that he know God's will for his life. It is the business of New Testament churches to plant God's message in the hearts and lives of individuals.

Nothing requires more skill and preparation than does "rightly dividing the word of truth." No one should stop short of the very best preparation for this the greatest of all tasks. Preachers, teachers, and workers in a church ought to do their utmost to qualify as teachers. To teach the Bible adequately to the lost and to those who have been won to Christ is big business. This is a big part of the work of evangelism.

When new converts are adequately taught the great doctrines of the Bible, results will be seen in their lives. Only eternity, however, will reveal the value and the outcome of the work of a teacher, with an open Bible every Sunday morning, in a room with, perhaps, eight or ten boys or girls, or with a class of adult men or women. Let no man or woman count it a small thing to have this privilege. "Teaching them to observe all things whatsoever I have commanded you" is a divine command yet a glorious privilege. Through its Sunday school a church can best meet this obligation.

2. *The Sunday School Is Adequate to Inform the Church Members*

The more people are informed, the better they respond. Sometimes people do not do because they do not know. Every member of a New Testament church should be thoroughly familiar with the entire program of the church. Since the New Testament church is a democracy, every member should have a vital part in the program.

Every member of a church should be enlisted in all the regular activities of the church. He should be informed regarding the special missionary activities. The financial policy and program should be thoroughly understood, and wholeheartedly participated in, by every member. By using the Sunday school, a church can see that new members have the facts about the financial program presented or explained to them. The same is true of other phases of the church life. If rightly used, the Sunday school is adequate to inform every member about the whole church program.

3. *The Sunday School Teaches Individual Responsibility*

More than half the members of Southern Baptist churches have never come to feel their share of the weight of their church program. They have taken responsibility so lightly.

Too often this has been the result of failure on the part of a church to educate the members to know their responsibility and their duties toward their church.

A church offers many rights and benefits, blessings and privileges. A person who belongs to a Baptist church should accept the blessings, but he should accept the responsibilities and obligations that go along with them. It is the duty of a church to see to it that each individual accepts his part of the responsibility of carrying on the program of Jesus Christ at home and around the world. At this point too many churches have failed. As a result, more than half of the people in Southern Baptist churches never contribute to the support of the work. They are not enlisted in the financial program. They do not attend its services. They are lost to the cause. Could it be that we have failed "to teach them to observe all things"?

Every member of a church should be taught to appreciate the rights and benefits of church membership. A well-organized Sunday school class can and does develop this appreciation. The class Standard and the Six Point Record System, if properly used, will lead members of a class to become conscious of the duty of a Christian to his church. Hundreds of people could testify to the value of a Sunday school class and what it has meant to them, in helping them to know Christ and his will for their lives.

VI. The Sunday School Can Utilize Those Won to Christ

The Great Commission is not finished when people are led to accept Christ as Saviour. Not until the church teaches the saved to observe all things whatsoever Christ has commanded is the task complete (Matt. 28:20). There has been failure at this point. Southern Baptist churches have had considerable success in the initial step of winning the lost to Christ. However, no one can boast about the way we have utilized those we have won.

The Sunday school, rightly used, is adequate to enlist and use all the people won. There are more than a million officers and teachers in the Sunday schools of the Southern Baptist Convention. In no other way have we been able, as yet, to put to work so many people. These officers and teachers are constantly at work training those enlisted in the Sunday school.

The Sunday school is the teaching agency of the church. It majors in teaching one thing—the Bible. Through the Sunday school, because of its constituency, a church reaches more people than in any other known way. The Sunday school can enlist more people to become faithful to their stewardship responsibility than any other agency of the church. Only the Sunday school has in it, or should have, all the members of the Baptist Training Union, all the members of the Woman's Missionary Union, and all the members of the Brotherhood. It evidently has in it the possibility for a program of perennial evangelism.

God has a place of service for every Christian. There is need, in the program of God, for every member of his family. God has a place of service for everyone. It is the business of a New Testament church to seek to get each member serving in the proper place.

In most churches a few people do all the work. The load of responsibility is borne by too few. Yet most of the others will respond if and when the right approach is made. Something needs to be done to utilize more of the people in the churches. "Everybody" ought to be "somebody" in a Baptist church. This means that everybody ought to be responsible for something in his church. Responsibility can and should be distributed.

People will serve if given an opportunity to do so. Evidently, people need to be taught "to observe all things," or Jesus would not have included teaching in his program for the church. Let us give serious consideration to it. And when we do, multitudes of people in our churches will not be standing by idle. They will go to work. Evangelism is not finished until the evangelized become evangelists. There is yet work to be done. The Sunday school will do its part when rightly used.

VII. The Sunday School Excels in Evangelism

The major work of a church has been briefly outlined in the preceding paragraphs. Now suppose we measure the Sunday school of a church to see just how adequate it is to reach people for Christ. Many New Testament churches have found that the Sunday school is adequate. It excels in many things if fully used.

1. It Locates the People to Be Reached

Sunday school workers have learned how to find those who are not, but who need to be, in Sunday school. This is the first step toward reaching them. Not only do Sunday school workers know how, but they are willing and ready to go into the highways and hedges to do so.

2. It Enlists People in Bible Study

People can be enlisted for Bible study. This, of course, is true only when the Sunday school is organized for it, when space is provided, when workers are trained for the task, when prospects are properly assigned, and when a regular program of visitation is maintained.

3. It Teaches the Scriptures Regularly

The Bible is the textbook of the Sunday school. The chief purpose of Southern Baptist Sunday schools is to teach the Bible. The Sunday school is equipped for this very thing. It is at its best when teaching. The record reveals that about as many are won to Christ each year as the net gain in Sunday school enrolment. About 90 per cent of all our baptisms come through the Sunday schools. This reveals the value of the Bible-teaching program of a church.

4. It Wins the Lost to Christ Week by Week

In a constantly growing Sunday school those to be won are in attendance. The gospel, which is the power of God unto salvation, is the message of the Sunday school. Officers and teachers in the Sunday school are some of the best soul-winners. This makes the Sunday school adequate for soul-winning. Churches need not gather together a few people and designate the soul-winning of the church to them. The Sunday school officers and teachers are at this task week by week. They are in closest touch with lost people. Most of the soul-winning done in the average church is done by the officers and teachers of the Sunday school.

5. *It Builds the Sunday Morning Congregation*

The Sunday school can and does put church members and lost people into the worship service. Children, as well as adults and young people, coming from the Sunday school into the preaching service on Sunday morning offer great evangelistic opportunities. It is commonly agreed that 90 per cent of an average Sunday morning congregation come through the Sunday school. Most of the young church members are in Sunday school, and they can be influenced to remain for the worship service.

Many things have been tried, but the best, surest way to have a good Sunday morning congregation every Sunday, year after year, is to use the Sunday school to do it. A quotation from Dr. Burroughs would be helpful at this point.

The Sunday school offers a valuable means of building a congregation. As the preaching service may make large contribution to the success of the teaching service, so the teaching service may lend aid in making the preaching service effective.

An able and successful pastor, whose praise is in all of the churches, bears the following witness:

"I can draw a crowd to my church any Sunday morning by announcing an unusual and sensational subject; I can repeat this for the evening hour. I can do the same the next Sunday. I can draw a crowd by announcing a program of attractive music. I have in the back of my head many ideas for the drawing of crowds; I have tested them and I know that they will work. But as the years pass, I grow dissatisfied with mere crowds and I long for a congregation, a sure and dependable congregation which will persist winter and summer, when I am in my pulpit and when I am not. I have deliberately and finally concluded that if I want a dependable congregation I must build a Sunday school organization. I have not always held this view. I did not come hastily to this position. I was forced to it, partly by my own experience, partly by observation and chiefly by an analytical study of the problem. The logic of the situation is clear and inescapable. A live and active Sunday school is the best and surest of all congregation builders."

Practically without exception the pastors who preach to large and interested congregations are the pastors who have built efficient Sunday schools. The numbers which attend upon the teaching ministry of many churches are quite as large as the numbers which attend upon the preaching ministry. In large measure, the secret of the large congregations which wait upon the pulpit ministry lies in the fact that goodly numbers are drawn to the church plant for the teaching service and that the faithful Sunday school workers busy themselves with the effort to keep the people for the preaching service which follows. It is not really a question whether the people will come to hear the preaching; it is rather a question whether being already in the building the people will remain for public worship and then hear the pastor's message.

Another minister who preaches to overflowing congregations bears this significant testimony:

"Some people give me credit for being an attractive preacher; it is true that large numbers wait on my ministry. The explanation is simple and very easy; our Sunday school draws upwards of a thousand people to our building every Sunday morning. When the Sunday school closes its service, some two hundred officers and workers in the Sunday school are alert, seeking to induce the people to remain to hear me preach."

The pastor added with a smile that any man who could not get a congregation with that backing ought not to try to preach. "Why," he said, "a wooden man ought to command a fair audience under such conditions."[1]

Teachers and officers will respond to the sympathetic, understanding, compassionate heart of a pastor in an urgent appeal for their co-operation in this matter.

[1] P. E. Burroughs, *Growing a Church* (Nashville: Broadman Press, 1927), pp. 87–88 (out of print).

6. *The Sunday School Builds a Great Financial Program for a Church*

Nothing will take the place of the Sunday school in enlisting all the members of a church in the financial support of the church program at home and around the world. Through the use of the Sunday school a church can subscribe and gather in the budget offerings better than any other way.

7. *It Helps a Pastor to Keep in Touch with and Use His People*

Churches do not lose people they use. The Sunday school offers places of service for most of the people. The Sunday school offers a pastor a practical, workable means of keeping in touch with all his people. In the Sunday school there are workers for every age group. There can and should be a worker for every ten to twenty persons for whom the pastor is responsible. Through the best use of his Sunday school, he can know and be able to minister to the needs of all his people. In no other way does this seem possible. Every officer and teacher is an associate to the pastor if allowed to be.

8. *The Sunday School Will Build a Great Church*

To build a great Sunday school is to build a great church. This is possible with every pastor. It should be the desire of everyone. When tested, successful methods of building a great Sunday school are used, a great church is the result. We have heard Dr. E. Hermond Westmoreland, pastor of South Main Baptist Church, Houston, Texas, say several times, "Build a great Sunday school and your Sunday school will build your church." How true this statement is!

9. *The Sunday School Is a Channel Through Which to Start New Work*

There are willing people in every congregation who will go out into other areas and start new Sunday schools if the pastor and people will find the locations and sponsor the work. Great progress in this direction is being made by many of the churches. It is nothing unusual today for a church to sponsor from one to five branch Sunday schools.

10. *All Sunday School Work Is for Evangelism*

Whether taking a census, building space for Bible study, grading Adults, going after people, teaching the Bible, training workers, or winning people to Christ, New Testament evangelism is at the heart of it all. The Sunday school does all of these things if rightly used. All good Sunday school work is evangelism.

Churches need no new soul-winning organization to win souls. The Sunday school is, and has, just what is needed. The officers and teachers are trained to do soul-winning, and in the average church most of it is done by Sunday school workers. A pastor who wants a soul-winning band needs only to use his officers and teachers.

The Sunday school rightly organized and functioning provides the best soul-winning opportunities. It has the information about every prospect for evangelism and church membership in the community. It has enrolled in its departments and classes the best prospects for evangelism. The contact has been made, the Bible has been taught, the soil has been prepared, and the harvest is certain if, and when, a church will seek to get the most out of the Sunday school.

QUESTIONS FOR REVIEW

1. Define perennial evangelism.

2. Why is the Sunday school adequate for perennial evangelism?

3. In what ways can the Sunday school be of help to a pastor in evangelism?

7

The Pastor and Perennial Evangelism

"And he gave some, apostles; and some, prophets; and some, evangelists; and some, pastors and teachers; for the perfecting of the saints, for the work of the ministry, for the edifying of the body of Christ: till we all come in the unity of the faith, and of the knowledge of the Son of God, unto a perfect man, unto the measure of the stature of the fulness of Christ" (Eph. 4:11–13).

THE PASTOR, more than any other human being, is responsible for the success or failure of his church. He is the key worker of his church—with emphasis on *worker,* for that he must be if he gets others to work. All church work should be Bible centered. Evangelism should be the central note in it all. If evangelism is to be kept central and at the heart of all Sunday school work, the pastor must see to it. Evangelistic pastors will have evangelistic Sunday schools.

All Sunday school work is for evangelism. Southern Baptists should start 25,000 additional Sunday schools, mission stations, and churches in the immediate future. Pastors, more than anyone else, can lead churches to do this. There are pastors who could start one or more Sunday schools—and they would, but they are afraid that it will hurt the mother church. Others have proved that this is not the case. New work never hurts, but helps, the sponsoring church.

I. Pastors Are Called and Commissioned

Men choose professions. God calls preachers. Churches also call preachers. The relationship of a pastor and his people is a sacred one—God's man working with God's people. God's man has a definite place today.

The phrase "man of God" is used over and over in the Bible to identify God-called men. Moses was spoken of as "man of God." Elijah was called "man of God." The apostle Paul called young Timothy "man of God." It was said that Samuel, "man of God, is in this city and he is held in honor."

1. Called to Preparation

Pastors must study the Bible. The Bible is the message that God wants men to have. One could never master all the message of the Book, even though he studied it every day of his life. It should be the chief aim and desire of a pastor to know what the "thus saith God" is for his people.

Pastors must study people. No one needs to know better how to be of help than does a pastor. It should be his sincere desire to be a constant blessing and help to those about him. To be able to do so, he must be a student of people. Human nature is a peculiar thing, and a pastor must, somehow or other, be able to understand it as fully as possible.

Pastors should study methods. No pastor should stop short of seeking to know the best, tested, tried, and proved methods in growing a great church. Every pastor will find it a most profitable investment of time to study methods.

Pastors should endeavor to keep themselves spiritually fit. Such endeavor is a must if the pastor is to keep the right spirit in his everyday life, in his outlook, and in his leadership. When spirituality is low, everything else will be low. Power will go from one when spirituality is gone. What the world needs today, and what God is calling for, is Spirit-filled men of God.

The admonition of Dr. George W. Truett to young preachers was, "Young men, stay on your knees and wallow in the Word." "But we will give ourselves continually to prayer, and to the ministry of the word" (Acts 6:4). The chief business of a God-called man is prayer and the ministry of the

Word of God. Let no pastor play loose with his God-given task.

2. Called to Preach

Preachers are called to preach! Jesus came preaching. God commanded Jonah, "Go . . . preach . . . the preaching that I bid thee." The power of the preaching of the preacher lies in the depth of his spiritual life. People will not excuse the man in the pulpit if he fails to preach. "It pleased God by the foolishness of preaching to save them" (1 Cor. 1:21).

If a preacher's preaching is to be what it ought to be, people must be gathered together to hear it. Nothing can be more helpful to a pastor at this point than his Sunday school. Lost people and prospects for church membership will be in his congregation on Sunday if he uses his Sunday school as he should.

The Sunday school puts both church members and lost people into the worship service. The children, young people, and adults coming directly from the Sunday school into the worship service on Sunday morning will offer a great evangelistic opportunity to any pastor. Most of the young church members are in the Sunday school, and they can be influenced to remain for the worship services.

Every pastor should take advantage of the evangelistic opportunities in the Sunday morning worship hour. Teachers and officers will respond to the sympathetic, understanding, compassionate appeal of the pastor. If called upon to do so, they will do their best to put the people into the preaching and worship service.

3. Called to Increase the Flock

The pastor is responsible for reaching people. "Say not ye, There are yet four months, and then cometh harvest? behold, I say unto you, Lift up your eyes, and look on the fields; for they are white already to harvest" (John 4:35). "And the lord said unto the servant, Go out into the highways and hedges, and compel them to come in, that my house may be filled" (Luke 14:23).

The task of every pastor is to get the unreached people enlisted in Bible study. The Sunday school is available and adequate for this task. The proper use of the Sunday school will make small churches large, and large churches larger. The pastor who wants to reach people and reach them fast must come to realize the value of his Sunday school.

The Sunday school is organized to reach people. No group in the world can locate people who are to be reached as can Sunday school officers and teachers. Educational buildings, if built right, make it easier to reach more people and reach them faster. Most people enlisted in Bible study in Southern Baptist churches are won to Christ within a reasonable time.

A well-organized Sunday school, fully graded on the age basis, with well-trained, consecrated teachers and officers, is the best available help a pastor has in reaching the people for whom he is responsible. Since it is the business of the pastor to increase the flock, surely he will use his Sunday school to the best advantage to do this very thing. A pastor can multiply his ministry hundreds of times through his Sunday school officers and teachers.

Dr. J. M. Frost, in his book *The School of the Church,* has much to say about the pastor and his "college of teachers." He gives a picture of a church school with the pastor teaching his officers and teachers to go out and reach people. More will be said about this later.

The pastor can increase the flock faster if he extends one or more arms out from his church in different directions. Branch Sunday schools reach people much faster than older ones. No pastor can afford to be without a mission Sunday school.

4. Called to Shepherd the Flock

What a beautiful picture the Bible uses for the relationship of pastor and people! A pastor of a church is to his people what a shepherd is to his flock. God's man has a definite place in service and ministry to God and to man. People have lost heart; the pastor is to encourage them. Some have doubts; he is to bring hope. The world is in sorrow; God's man is to give comfort. People have stumbled; he is to lift the fallen.

There are so many things that a shepherd of a flock does. He feeds his sheep; he cares for them. He tries to see that their needs, physical and spiritual, are met inasmuch as it is possible for him to do so.

Someone has said that the shepherd must also "shear" the flock. Sheep will lose or ruin a valuable part of their wool unless it is taken from them at certain seasons of the year. Too many of God's people misspend God's money unless the shepherd of the flock gives diligence to this particular responsibility of tending the sheep. The pastor should see to it that his church has a good financial program. He should endeavor to enlist every member of his church to be faithful in his Christian stewardship.

5. *Called to Teach*

Pastors are called also to teach. The Scriptures describe it in this wise—"apt to teach." "Teaching them to observe all things whatsoever I have commanded you" is the word of God to his servants. Evidently, some pastors have not recognized "teaching" as a part of their duty. Paul gave much of his time to this great ministry.

Jesus spent three years teaching men how and what to teach. He gathered around himself a group who would help carry on the work. He spent three years, prior to his death, teaching the twelve.

Trained workers make better workers. The success of a pastor depends largely upon his ability to gather about him a group of officers and teachers and train them to do what needs to be done. He must teach teachers. The people are willing, but they must be taught how to do that which they are expected to do. Any pastor can multiply himself through teaching others.

Surely Dr. J. M. Frost was right at the heart of this great matter when he spoke of the possibilities of a pastor with his "college of teachers" multiplying himself by the right use of them. He said, "The pastor has his empire in the service of teaching his teachers." [1] Again he said: "Here he makes full proof of his ministry, to the honor and glory of his Master. His church, as a field, will be white unto harvest, ready for the reaper's sickle; as a force, it will be mighty for God and for doing things in the kingdom; as a field, it will have always the joyous music of those who harvest the golden grain; as a force, it will have the shout of triumph like the victor's song; as a field, this pastor and his church will come rejoicing, bringing in the sheaves; as a force, they will come as the conquering army comes with trophies for the King and new conquests for his crown." [2]

II. PASTORS ARE ALSO PASTORS OF THEIR SUNDAY SCHOOLS

By virtue of his call, the pastor is the divinely appointed leader of every unit in the church to which he has been called. The Sunday school is a church agency, and it should be used for everything for which it is adequate. The success of a Sunday school will be in proportion to the vision the pastor has for it and the faith he has in it. He must lift the vision of the workers of his church and Sunday school. More and more the Sunday school is coming to be recognized as a means by which a pastor will multiply himself over and over.

Pastors get big dividends in return for every effort spent in Sunday school work. In most instances, other leaders in the church will not go beyond the pastor. For his Sunday school to be a success, he must plan for it and then lead his people to accomplish the plans. There is no short cut in building bigger and better Sunday schools. This requires hard work. The pastor must be one of the workmen, and he must put many others to work.

1. *Must Enlist and Encourage Workers*

In some churches it has been difficult to enlist and train enough capable workers for a successful Sunday school. But

---

[1] Frost, J. M., *The School of the Church* (New York: Fleming H. Revell Company, 1911) p. 107 (out of print). Used by permission.
[2] *Ibid*, pp. 108–109.

this is necessary, and pastors must keep at it. The pastor, in co-operation with the superintendent and educational director, if he has one, must enlist and put enough capable workers to work to reach the unreached for Bible study. When the hands of the pastor are tied by "top-heavy" organization which limits his direct contact with his Sunday school and other church agencies, the work is handicapped. He, better than any other, should know what should be done and when to do it.

Selecting and training workers is one of the pastor's most fruitful fields of labor, and his responsibility should not be taken from him; neither should anything be allowed to come in the way. To maintain a ready supply of workers, regular training opportunities must be provided. The pastor is responsible for this.

Workers need encouragement from the pastor. Frequent recognition of faithful and successful efforts should be given those who labor in the Sunday school. A few words of commendation from the pastor will mean much to a worker. Such recognition will also magnify and dignify the Sunday school work in the thinking of the workers, and in the minds of other members of the church.

The relationship between the pastor and other workers in the Sunday school must be a happy one. There can be no followship without leadership. The right kind of leadership always produces good followship. A compassionate-hearted pastor who trains his workers and works at the task with them can inspirit team play and a happy, wholesome relationship. Wise and happy is the pastor who puts ten people to work rather than attempting to do the work of ten people. The pastor and his workers are co-laborers in a common task with and for God. They should have frequent conferences concerning the work. Planning precedes progress.

2. Must Lead the School to "Move Up"—in Organization

The pastor must be able to depend upon the superintendent of the Sunday school for the work that must be done, but the pastor's guidance, counsel, and leadership should be available at all times. He should be the pastor of the Sunday school and see that things go as they should. He must furnish both vision and faith for the program.

Every New Testament church is in a spiritual conquest. This calls for reaching people. Some things are absolutely essential to reaching people for Christ. The pattern of the Sunday school determines the reach. For a church to keep on growing, the pattern must be enlarged frequently. The pastor's vision for his Sunday school and his knowledge of best methods of reaching people will determine how well he leads his church in an expanding organization.

Enlarge the pattern from a class to a department Sunday school. Few class Sunday schools ever average better than 150 in attendance. The class pattern should be stepped up. The pastor, more than any other person, can lead his church to "move up." Growth demands a larger pattern. Churches, to grow, must keep stepping up the pattern.

Sunday schools saturate. Growth slows down, even ceases. Unless the pattern is enlarged, there will be no more growth. A Sunday school with only one department for each age group can reach so many people and no more. Before the ratio between the number enrolled and the number of workers begins to approach the well-known "ten to one," enlarge the pattern by enlisting more workers. Start more departments and more classes.

It may be that your Sunday school needs to move up from one department to two, in at least some age groups. It could be that your Sunday school is one that should move up to multiple departments for each age group. It has been proved that more departments, more classes, and more workers will reach more people.

Keep your Sunday school graded, Pastor, both by age and sex, if you desire best results.

3. *Must Lead the School to "Move On"—in Training*

The average church has by far too few workers to do the task that ought to be done. The key to having plenty of workers is a well-wrought-out churchwide training program.

A more complete discussion on this subject can be found in chapter 5. A pastor can and must lead his people to train. No one can take his place nor his responsibility when it comes to training those who would serve him.

4. *Must Lead the School to "Move In"—Additional Space*

Much needs to be said about the need for, and the value of, additional space in most Baptist churches. Baptists have found that they can fill with people all the space that they are willing to build or provide. Churches reach as many people as they provide space to accommodate—no more, and no less. Pastors realize this truth more and more as they try to reach people.

Space holds the key; pastors must lead their people to provide it. Failure to do so hinders the program of Christ. The time to build is when space is needed. A church will never go beyond its leadership in this matter.

5. *Must Lead the School to "Move Out"—New Sunday Schools*

Unreached millions are out beyond the reach of existing churches. Additional churches must be started if ever these people are reached.

"A Church Without a Child Is Out of Style" is a timely slogan used by one association. One church, which is sponsoring a mission in its city, also underwrote a loan in Denver, Colorado, for a church to get under way with a building program. They ordained a young preacher and sent him to Boulder City, Nevada, to start and pastor another church there. There are thousands of places where a similar thing could be done.

6. *Must Lead the School to "Move Together"—in the Association*

Southern Baptists have discovered that through co-operation their churches can move together in a denominational program with great results. They have always

endeavored not only to reach every church in every association with the best possible program of work, but also to
provide a church within easy reach of every family. This
calls for a good associational program. Larger churches may
not need the help of the smaller churches, but the weaker
ones need the help of the stronger. It is wonderful to see
pastors of stronger churches leading their people to partici-
pate in the work of the district association. The pastor's interest in associational work will develop interest on the part
of his people.

III. Some Conclusions Are Evident

The pastor should lead his church to provide adequate
space and equipment to take care of every prospect for his
Sunday school. He, more than anyone else, is responsible to
see that enough new classes and departments are started to
provide adequately the necessary organization to reach the
people.

The pastor must see that the church keeps on enlisting
and training more workers. He should see that adequate
training opportunities are offered, so that workers may be
unashamed and ready to do the task.

The pastor must lead the church to magnify a program
of visitation. Nothing short of this will build a great church.

The pastor must lead his church to realize the true value
of the Six Point Record System, and to become efficient in
its use. Successful churches have found that this gives ex-
cellent direction for the work.

The pastor should lead the church to adopt the Standards
of Excellence as the program for all units in the Sunday
school. Working through the superintendent and educational director, he should lead the school to follow this program. The nearer Standard a school is, the better its work.

The pastor must promote grading and promotion. Beyond
any doubt, Sunday schools that are thoroughly graded by
age and sex do better work, and produce better results in
evangelism.

The pastor, more than anyone else, is the key to a successful weekly officers and teachers' meeting. This meeting is essential to keeping the whole Sunday school at work in the whole program of evangelism.

The pastor must see the need, if the babies are to be adequately provided for, and if the Cradle Roll and Nursery departments are to go as they should.

Pastors can use their Sunday schools in special revival crusades to a great advantage. The Sunday school, better than any other agency, can put prospects into the revival services. Sunday school officers and teachers should be used by the pastor during special revival efforts as well as throughout the year.

The pastor should give himself fully to the Vacation Bible school during the season for it. Two weeks cannot be spent in any other way that will bring about the lasting good that Vacation Bible school does. This is one of a church's greatest opportunities for evangelism.

Pastors who give strong emphasis to the associational program and meetings will lead their churches to respond in a marvelous way. The strong churches should put forth special efforts to strengthen the associational organization so that help can be given to all the churches. As goes the pastor's spirit in this matter, so will go his church.

People should know, and they do, what a pastor thinks of his Sunday school.

Dr. George W. Truett said many times, "Next to the wife of my heart, next to the children God has given me, I hold dear the company of men and women who teach in my Sunday school."

The pastor who puts little into his Sunday school will get little results from it. Again we quote from Dr. P. E. Burroughs' book *Growing a Church:* "The pastor who without stint gives himself to his Sunday school; the pastor who sends his faith and his spirit down through the entire Sunday school organization; the pastor who takes time to teach and train his teachers; such pastor will not find any failure on the part of his Sunday school officers and teachers and pupils to support his preaching ministry." [3]

QUESTIONS FOR REVIEW

1. What one person, more than any other, is responsible for the success or failure of his church?

2. What are the chief duties of a pastor?

3. What is the relationship between a pastor and the Sunday school?

[3] P. E. Burroughs, *Growing a Church* (Nashville: Broadman Press, 1927) p. 89.

8

Special Efforts in Evangelism

> "If my people, which are called by my name, shall humble themselves, and pray, and seek my face, and turn from their wicked ways; then will I hear from heaven, and will forgive their sin, and will heal their land" (2 Chron. 7:14).

EVERYTHING that a church does should be for evangelism. There is a time and place in a church for special revival effort. Some people can be reached through special crusades who could not be reached otherwise.

I. GETTING READY FOR A CRUSADE

General Eisenhower said to his men just before the European invasion, "There is no easy way to win a war." The same thing may be said about a revival. The recipe for revivals is found fully outlined in the Scripture passage at the beginning of this chapter.

1. Explore the Possibilities for a Crusade

Get acquainted with the possibilities of the crusade. Revival is a time to meet spiritual needs. There needs to be a great turning to God and his way of life on the part of many cold and indifferent Christians. Baptists who are detached from their churches because of distance should be enlisted in active duty for Christ in the community where they live. There are more unsaved people in every community than the average church member would believe. Nothing short of a house-to-house search for them will reveal the possibilities for evangelism. Every church should make a thorough religious survey of the community in preparation for the revival meeting. The Sunday school is available and adequate to make this survey. For details about taking a census see *Building a Standard Sunday School* by Arthur Flake or *A Church Using Its Sunday School* by J. N. Barnette.

2. Enlarge the Sunday School Organization

Many evangelists and pastors have found it to be a wise thing to have a good enlargement campaign in a church about four to six months before the special revival effort, as a major part of the preparation for the revival. This puts the evangelistic possibilities into classes for Bible study, getting their hearts ready for special decisions during the campaign.

With the information found from the census and the present Sunday school enrolment before you, plan the needed number of units, departments, and classes based on the laws of Sunday school growth.

The following chart will help you decide on the number of classes needed:

Age Group Involved	A Class Is Needed for Every	
Adult Men	10–40	Possibilities
Adult Women	10–40	"
Married Young Men	8–20	"
Married Young Women	8–20	"
Single Men 19–24	8–20	"
Single Women 19–24	8–20	"
Single Men 17 and 18 years	8–15	"
Single Girls 17 and 18 years	8–15	"
Intermediate Boys 13–16	6–8	"
Intermediate Girls 13–16	6–8	"
Junior Boys 9–12	6–8	"
Junior Girls 9–12	6–8	"
Primary Children 6–8	6–8	"
Beginner Children 4–5	5–7	"
Nurseries (children under 4)	4 or more Nurseries	
Cradle Roll Visitors	3 for every 100 church members	
Extension Department Visitors	3 for every 100 church members	

For more detailed information see *The Pull of the People* by Dr. J. N. Barnette.

3. Enlist and Train Additional Workers

Information on this point may be found in another chapter in this book.

4. Assign Pupils and Prospects

See that a list of pupils and prospects is put into the hands of the superintendent and teacher responsible for each age group. A copy of the entire list of prospects should be on file in the church office. One should be available for use by the pastor. An up-to-date list of all prospects should be made available to the evangelist who is to direct the revival campaign if he should request it.

5. Enrol the Prospects in Sunday School

The best available way known to condition unsaved people for spiritual decisions is Bible study in a Sunday school class.

6. Write Letters to Prospects

A personal letter sent to every prospect soon after the census will prove most helpful. Some pastors plan for each prospect to get a letter from him on Thursday before the revival begins on Sunday, one from the Sunday school superintendent on Friday, and then one from the teacher on Saturday. A piece of attractive publicity of the revival should be enclosed in each letter.

7. Send a Letter from the Evangelist to the Workers

The writer has found it most helpful when he serves as evangelist, to have a list of all the church-elected officers and teachers sent to him at least two weeks before the revival. A personal letter from the visiting evangelist to the workers in a church about the plans for the revival, and how each one can be most helpful in the special quest for souls, will be worth far more than the trouble and cost.

8. *Sign Up the Workers*

At least a month before the crusade, the pastor and other Sunday school officers should begin an effort to get every worker and every member of the Sunday school and of the church committed to 100 per cent attendance on every service. The teacher who pledges to attend will have no difficulty in getting the pupils pledged to do so.

A special crusade calls for "everyone's best." The people will sign up to be present if challenged to do so. Many churches fail to realize the value of the Sunday school in putting people (lost and saved) into every service. The Sunday school may be used only one week or it may be used during the entire crusade. The record sheet shown on the following page has proved helpful in securing commitments. This blank provides a complete record for attendance throughout one week. The blank should be adapted to the length of time the Sunday school is used in the crusade.

The following blank, or something similar, may be given to each person in attendance each night to be filled in and handed to the class secretary.

SUNDAY SCHOOL AT NIGHT

(Individual Report Blank)

Name _____ John Doe _____ Date __ April 10 __

Member of this church   Yes_____   No_____

Member of this Sunday school   Yes_____   No_____

I belong to the_____ Church_____
                  (Denomination)   (Address)

NAME OF THE CHURCH

REVIVAL

Thumbnail-
sized picture,
or name only
if mimeo-
graphed.

(Date)

Same as
other
side.

Evangelist   **Singer**

Since my church is in an all-out quest for souls, and because of my love for Christ and lost people, I pledge to be present at every service unless providentially hindered.

I will be present also for the special periods "Sunday School at Night."

Department_____ Class (Age_____) (Sex_____)

	M	T	W	TH	F	S	
Teacher							
Pupil							

Of course, the suggested blanks should be adapted to meet the needs of the given situation. Following is a blank to be used for a quick report for promotional purposes at the beginning of the revival service each night:

SUNDAY SCHOOL AT NIGHT

(Class Report Blank)

Department _____Adult I_____ Date __April 10__

Class _____Ladies 30–31 years_____

Teacher _____Mrs. John Doe_____

Members Present _____7_____

Prospects: Unaffiliated _____5_____

Unsaved _____2_____

Total Present _____14_____

Something similar to the foregoing blank, with necessary changes, may be used for the department report.

9. *Lead the People to Pray for the Crusade*

Prayer causes people to become conscious of their need for revival. When Christians pray, they begin to get right with God; when Christians get right with God, they become burdened for the lost; when they become burdened for the lost, the Holy Spirit begins convicting the lost of their sins, and revival is on.

Several weeks before the crusade starts, special prayer meetings should be held in homes, shops, stores, factories, business houses, and everywhere a group of people can be gathered day or night. Little prayer will not produce great revivals. Many churches have found "around-the-clock" prayer for revival helpful.

10. *Publicize the Campaign*

Start early and publicize the crusade in every way possible. Use the newspapers, handbills, posters, cards, letters, radio, television, streamers, billboards, car-bumper stickers, and other available means. Revival signs on taxicabs and city buses are most powerful. Do not leave undone anything that might be helpful.

11. *Plan Special Visitation*

See that a copy of the prospect list is put into the hands of those responsible for each age group. The pastor should have a copy, and one should be put into the hands of the evangelist.

Make out a card for each prospect, to be used in special visitation assignments before and during the crusade. Use the best-known method for promoting visitation during the revival.

II. DURING THE CRUSADE

Exploring the possibilities for using the Sunday school during the revival is a tremendous task, but it is worth everything that it takes to do it. Preparation is essential to revival. After preparation is made, the procedure followed during revival is of vital importance.

1. *Have Sunday School Every Night*

If the Sunday school is properly organized, then charged and challenged with the responsibility, the house will be filled for every service during a revival. The Sunday school is adequate to do this. Each person is responsible for a few. No one is responsible for too many—another good reason for small classes.

Where adequate preparation has been made for its use, "Sunday School at Night" has proved most successful in putting prospects into revival services. It works in large or small churches.

For several years a little rural church in one of the Southern states had eight or nine classes in its Sunday school, with an average attendance of about sixty to sixty-five. This writer was invited to that church for an enlargement campaign. After the census returns were fully graded, he began talking for a department school, because a class school could not minister adequately to their prospects.

Someone from the floor suggested that it would be impossible because they could not get the workers. Another suggested that the space they had would not lend itself to a department Sunday school. But they all finally agreed to permit the pastor, the superintendent, and the visiting preacher to work out the problem of workers and space during the next day.

The next day, Saturday, no time was lost. The pastor, the superintendent, and the visitor worked hard. The floor space was studied and rearranged. Thirty-five workers were enlisted. A department organization was set up on paper. The prospects were assigned to the proper classes. Teachers and officers went to work Saturday afternoon after they had been enlisted.

Saturday night, when the enlarged plan was presented to the church to be voted on, someone laughed and said: "That sounds good, but where will we get the thirty-five workers that the new plan calls for?" That fellow did not know it, but those thirty-five workers had been enlisted and they were present. When asked to do so, those who had accepted places of responsibility stood. When thirty-five people stood to their feet, the congregation was amazed.

The church voted reluctantly to try the enlarged program. New locations were assigned, and plans were made for Sunday morning. Sunday morning came. Thirty-five workers were ready. When the reports were in, it was discovered that 105 people were present.

That was the first day for the Sunday school to meet by departments. Some of the people were taken around to see the situation—some who had been skeptical. Some suggested that the arrangement seemed to be better by departments than it had been by classes. They were reminded that there were 105 people in the space instead of the 60 to 65 that ordinarily they had. The people could hardly believe it. The pastor and superintendent were overwhelmed.

The next day, Monday, the revival started in that little Baptist church—really the revival had started with the enlargement campaign. The evangelist knew that the church had just moved up from a class to a department school. He understood thoroughly the purpose of the enlarged organization. He knew how to use the Sunday school in the revival. He challenged those officers and teachers of the Sunday school to have the enrolment present every night during the week.

For thirty minutes each night before the revival services started, the Sunday school met just as on Sunday. Those new officers and teachers, along with the older ones, got busy. More people were present each night than they had enrolled in Sunday school previous to that time.

Sunday morning, eight days from the day they started by departments, instead of having 60 or 65 present, they had 184 people in Sunday school. Without additional space, that Sunday school had moved from 9 to 24 classes, and from 13 to 35 workers. The enrolment jumped that day from 131 to 204. More than that, they had 43 additions to that little church during that brief period of revival.

This reveals what can be done when the pattern is enlarged to meet the needs, and the organization is put to work. This writer has the conviction that a Sunday school, if challenged to do so, can do every night during a special quest for souls what it can do on Sunday morning. For several years he has repeatedly seen this very thing happen. He highly recommends it. Try it, but not without much prayer and preparation. It will not work itself. It works if worked.

2. Use the Telephones

When your evangelist arrives, have two telephone directories available to cut into pieces. Organize a telephone brigade and call every number in your community informing the people of, and inviting all of them to, the revival. Of course, in large cities and certain other areas, this may be impossible. If so have all the church members called.

3. Have a Meeting of All Church Workers

A meeting, not later than the first day of the campaign, of all workers of every agency of the church will prove most helpful. This is a time for instruction and prayer for the crusade. The program for the crusade should be thoroughly explained to everyone.

4. Send Visitation Teams

Special visitation, by teams of two each, for one hour before the Sunday school period each night, has been blessed on many occasions. Supper, of course, must be served at the church for the visitors. Each class of Adults, Young People, and Intermediates will provide at least two soul-winners every night during the revival for this special visitation. Commit them to do so.

Special assignments should be made to the teams at the supper meeting. Use every other available means of assigned visitation during the crusade. Most people must be won to Christ in the home or business place before they make their public decision.

5. Use the Baptistry Every Night During the Revival

This is one of the best means available to get whole families into the services. Many parents have been won to Christ during a revival who, earlier in the meeting, came to see a child baptized. Lost people and others will come to witness Bible baptism. The Holy Spirit will do his work when they come. This ordinance, when properly administered, visualizes a gospel message.

6. Set High Attendance Day

Sunday is the biggest day in most revivals. Designate "high attendance Sunday" and make the Sunday school responsible for getting the people to attend. If rightly used, the Sunday school can pack the church house with prospects. Many successful methods have been used to make the most of high attendance day in the Sunday school. Use the method you think most successful.

III. AFTER THE REVIVAL

Southern Baptists are strong on some phases of evangelism. Their program for finding, reaching, and winning people to Christ is the best plan known to religious groups. However, they have not been too successful in conserving their gains.

Dr. J. B. Gambrell once said, "We have evangelized and we have baptized, but we have not taught, and out of that has come most of our troubles."

Dr. William E. Hatcher likewise said, "It is as important to save what we have as it is to save the lost."

Dr. L. R. Scarborough, the great evangelist, said, "One hundred new converts are one hundred liabilities until they are assimilated into the life of a church."

1. *Use or Lose People*

A good slogan for a New Testament church is "Every Member Saved and Serving." "Teaching them to observe all things whatsoever I have commanded you" is a part of the church program of evangelism. The weakest place in the program of evangelism in most churches has been in conserving the gains. Therefore there are two million or more Southern Baptists who do not have their church membership in the community where they live.

A large percentage of resident members are not active in the program of their church. They do not give; they have never met the church treasurer; they only know the church clerk. They do not attend the services; they do not support the program. Churches should be as interested in people after they are saved as they are before. Yet all too many churches, when people come for membership, ask nothing of them except to "take a seat." They are never enlisted and used in service of any kind.

(1) *"Evangelism is not complete until the evangelized become evangelists."*—Bible evangelism does not stop at winning people to Christ. It stabilizes and utilizes those won until they actually become "doers of the word, and not hearers only." Evangelism starts with the individual where he is—lost and ruined because of sin—and follows through until he comes "unto the measure of the stature of the fulness of Christ" (Eph. 4:13).

Salvation of a soul is a definite, completed act that takes place in regeneration; salvation of a life is a continued process. Evangelism is not complete, then, until the one evangelized becomes Christlike and observes "all things whatsoever I have commanded you" (Matt. 28:20).

With this fact in mind, one might ask: "What has the Sunday school been doing while 2,460,437 nonresident people are lost to the cause, and another 25 per cent of the membership of Southern Baptist churches, although living in the communities where their membership is, never give, never attend, nor support the services of their respective churches?" The Baptist Training Union and other church organizations have conserved many for active service, but even so, more than 2,000,000 have been permitted to stray away.

(2) *Enlist and hold.*—New converts who are not enlisted and who do not become active in the organizations of a church during the first few weeks of their church life are most likely to become liabilities rather than assets. A new baby in a home brings added responsibility to parents. New members of a church must likewise be given special care and attention.

The main part of the responsibility for caring for the babes in Christ belongs to the pastor. However, the different organizations in the church will be of valuable help if the church has an adequate program for conserving the gains. There is nothing like the organizations of a New Testament church for conserving gains, if properly functioning. All too many churches have not used their existing organizations for this purpose.

2. *Enlarge Organization to Help Conserve Gains*

For months before a new baby comes into a home, things are made ready for his arrival. Everything necessary is done to give him a hearty reception. Provision is made for his needs. No less thought and care should be given new members who join a church. Plan for enlargement when you plan for revival.

Churches plan ways and means to get people to make the decision and to get them into the church during special revival efforts. But all too many do not plan a program of enlargement to hold, teach, train, and utilize new converts.

Along with our plans and preparation for revival, we should study the present organizations of the church with the view of enlarging to meet future needs. If necessary, new classes and unions should be started in the Sunday school and Training Union. New people should never be put in overcrowded classes and unions. Provide for them or lose them.

New people not enrolled in Sunday school, who come into our churches during revivals, and who are put into saturated classes and unions, will not be given the attention that new Christians need. Plan to enlarge your organization at revival time to take care of all new people who come into your church. All new members should be assigned to classes on the basis of their age and sex. New people need special care and attention. You can hold them if provision is made for them. Provide enough teaching units so that the classes to which the new people go will not be overcrowded or too large.

Pastor, when you begin planning your next revival, why not plan also for enlargement to hold those won during the revival? Some have found that one reason they have lost so many of the new converts was that the Sunday school classes and Training Unions were all filled and adequate provision was not made to hold new people.

There is no better time to enlist the new workers necessary for enlargement than during a revival. Evangelists will preach, pray, and work to help a pastor do this very thing.

3. *Make Church Membership Mean Something*

The time to start conserving gains is the moment one presents himself for membership in a church.

(1) *Properly receive new members.*—When new members are received into the fellowship of a church family, it should be understood by them that it is really something to belong to a Baptist church, that the church really has something to offer the members, and that something is expected of them.

Receiving new members should be made an impressive part of the service. It is no time for hurry. It can be a blessing to both old and new members. When a person walks down the aisle of a church and presents himself or herself to Jesus and for membership in a local assembly called a New Testament church, every member should rejoice. Something should be done about it. Much should be made over it.

Proper care should be taken in receiving members. The rights and benefits, the opportunities and blessings, along with the responsibilities, duties, and obligations of church membership, should be explained. The definite decision of the candidate should be made plain to the congregation. Careful, enthusiastic presentation of the one coming for membership should be made by the pastor, or the one in charge, to the church. Proper vote should be taken by the members of the church.

Care should be taken at the close of the service to greet and welcome properly all new members coming into the church. Those coming for baptism should be baptized as soon as possible. One of the most meaningful messages preached in a church is the ordinance of baptism, if properly explained and administered.

(2) *Adequately inform and instruct new members.*—It should be definitely explained to each new member that a

person coming into the membership of a New Testament church has something wonderful in store for him. Many are the blessings, privileges, and rights that the church has to offer the members of the church family. It should be thoroughly explained that these rights and benefits are available, but that each member must avail himself of them. Likewise, it should be made very clear that there are obligations, responsibilities, and duties that one should assume who comes into the fellowship of a New Testament church.

4. Orient New Members

Church membership is no light thing, and it should not be treated lightly. The church is a place for people to serve, to give, to benefit, not only themselves but the world. Many times people do not do because they do not know. Informed church members are better members. It should be made definitely clear to each new member on acceptance that he will be expected to become informed about the church program, to accept his duties and responsibilities as a member, and to avail himself of the blessings and opportunities which the church has to offer him.

(1) *Have a pastor's class.*—One of the first expressions of gratitude of a new Christian, to Christ who has saved him from sin, or of the Baptist who has just moved his membership, should be to enrol and attend faithfully an orientation class taught by the pastor of the church. This class may be a part of the Baptist Training Union that meets every Sunday night. The class should have in it, for the first five Sunday nights after he becomes a member, every person who joins the church. During this time the pastor will instruct new members in their duties, their responsibilities, and the privileges of the church. It is suggested that they study *Your Life and Your Church* by Dr. James L. Sullivan.

(2) *Make personal visits in the home.*—The pastor should visit in the home of every new member at the earliest date possible. At least one other visit should be made immediately by the proper team of visitors who should take a church packet to the new member. It should include a

church covenant; the various quarterlies to be used by the new member; a church directory, if available; a packet of offering envelopes with the Six Point Record System on them; a tither's card; a talent-search card; and any other item which the member needs in order to become identified with the church program. The church program should be explained and new members should be enlisted immediately in every phase of the work—the quicker the better. Too often those not enlisted immediately are never enlisted.

(3) *Do not delay baptism.*—Every candidate for baptism should be baptized as soon as possible after the decision is made. Soon after baptism the church should offer the opportunity to the new member to partake of the Lord's Supper. The pastor should thoroughly explain the ordinances to new members.

(4) *Assign a sponsor to each new member.*—Some pastors have found it very helpful to assign each new member to a sponsor. The older member will give special care and attention to the new one for a few weeks until he has become oriented and enlisted. This helps both the old and new member.

(5) *Have a reception for new members.*—At frequent intervals churches should have a reception for new members. This is a good place and time for the heads of the different organizations to inform new members about the work of each department and to get acquainted with them.

(6) *Make new members special guests.*—New members should be special guests at the different meetings of the church groups until they are made to feel a part of the church. At every meeting the fellowship should be such that new members feel welcome and happy.

(7) *Assign new members to the organizations.*—The church that has the Sunday school and the other organizations organized to use people has no trouble enlisting new members. If they are not already in a Sunday school class, the new members are assigned immediately to the proper age group and a teacher becomes responsible for enlistment. The same thing should be done in the Training Union

and in the W.M.U. or the Brotherhood. Churches do not lose people they use. A church has the right to expect something from those who make up its membership. Unless they are enlisted, they become liabilities.

QUESTIONS FOR REVIEW

1. Outline a good procedure for getting a church ready for a revival crusade.

2. How can the Sunday school best be used in a special quest for souls?

3. What can be done to help conserve the gains in a church?

9

Evangelism Includes New Work

Jesus said, "Let us go into the next towns, that I may preach there also" (Mark 1:38). He also said, "Lift up your eyes, and look on the fields; for they are white already to harvest" (John 4:35).

THE STATEMENT was made recently by an outstanding Christian leader that there are too many overchurched communities. That statement challenged the writer to find one such community. The search prompted him to believe that there are far too few churches to minister to the spiritual needs of the people. When is a community properly churched? When is one overchurched?

Most boys and girls and many adults who are not in Sunday school and church are living in the unchurched areas out beyond the practical reach of existing churches.

The business world will see to it that enough grocery and dry goods stores are started and operated to supply the demand. The devil will see to it that liquor stores and places of evil are within easy reach of every member of every family. How long will it remain true that the children of this world are wiser in their generation than the children of light? Churches need to start other churches.

If churches fail to "go tell," then the message will not be heard. Men will die in their sins; yet their blood God will require at the hands of those who withhold the good news. Is this not reason enough for putting a New Testament church within easy reach of everyone? Jesus gave the keys to his kingdom to his followers—those who constitute his church. He is not expecting some other agency or institution to bring in his kingdom. Churches are responsible to do that.

I. "REGIONS BEYOND" MUST BE CHURCHED

One morning after Jesus had been in prayer for hours, even before the dawn of day, Simon and some others sought him in behalf of the people of the community whose needs were urgent. In the face of local needs, where the demands were worthy and great, Jesus revealed to his followers that there were needs in regions beyond also that should be met (Mark 1:35–38).

On another occasion Jesus made it plain that his followers were to witness at the same time "in Jerusalem, and in all Judaea, and in Samaria, and unto the uttermost part of the earth" (Acts 1:8). We do no violence to the Word when we translate "both" to mean "at the same time."

Paul, in a letter to the church at Corinth, expressed the sincere desire of his heart that their field for preaching the gospel would be enlarged to take in districts beyond their local community (2 Cor. 10:15–16). Paul realized the need for planting a New Testament church in every unchurched community.

An associational missionary writes, "A new day has dawned in our association since so many new Sunday schools and churches have been started in unchurched communities of our territory."

Another said, "Each year our desire to place a church in every unchurched community seems to grow."

Churches are responsible for starting mission stations and New Testament churches, not only in communities where people are interested, but wherever there are people who need this ministry. It is the business of Christian people to help those who are not interested become interested. The best way we know to do this is to start a Sunday school or a mission station near them.

One church made the mistake of polling the people in a community to see whether they were interested in a branch Sunday school. Of course they were not interested. If they had been, they would not have needed the assistance of this church; they would have gone ahead and started one. This discouraged the church. The Sunday school was not started.

It costs something in money and service to reach people for Christ, but Southern Baptists have in their custody both time and money that belong to the Lord. There are many reasons for going into regions beyond.

1. The Call of the Lord of the Harvest

Mark recorded Jesus as saying, "Go ye into all the world, and preach the gospel to every creature" (Mark 16:15).

Luke reminds us that Jesus said unto them: "Thus it is written, and thus it behoved Christ to suffer, and to rise from the dead the third day: and that repentance and remission of sins should be preached in his name among all nations, beginning at Jerusalem. And ye are witnesses of these things" (Luke 24:46-48).

John will not let us get away from what Jesus said on the resurrection side of the grave: "Then said Jesus to them again, Peace be unto you: as my Father hath sent me, even so send I you. And when he had said this, he breathed on them, and saith unto them, Receive ye the Holy Ghost: whose soever sins ye remit, they are remitted unto them; and whose soever sins ye retain, they are retained" (John 20:21-23).

Could it be possible that one who has read these words could be careless and complacent when it is his responsibility to give to others the gospel of Jesus Christ? The destiny of unborn generations will be changed by what we do. The orders have been given. The power has been promised. The responsibility is upon us. The time to march is now. Let us go on into regions beyond because of the call of the Christ of the multitudes, the Lord of the harvest. This is surely the day for God's people to claim the multitudes for Christ.

2. The Macedonian Call

In the sixteenth chapter of the Acts of the Apostles, we read: "And a vision appeared to Paul in the night; There stood a man of Macedonia, and prayed him, saying, Come over into Macedonia, and help us" (v. 9).

Thousands have heard the Macedonian call since the day of the apostle Paul. One day a letter came to the church where this writer was pastor. It was signed by twenty-three people. The letter read: "We hear that the First Baptist Church is interested in lost people no matter where they live, or what side of the railroad track they are on. Will you give us a Sunday school?"

When the pastor read that letter, he went immediately to his study; he locked the door; he read the letter again; he got down on his knees and asked God to keep him on his face until he could get up with the conviction that the pastor of that church loved lost people, no matter where they lived, or on what side of the railroad track they were. This made a difference. He called the deacons of the church together. Eighteen of them came. They read the letter. Nineteen men got on their knees and pledged God their best in leading their church into a great mission program for Christ.

That pledge, I think, added to the future success of that church. Not only did the church respond to that appeal, but it was more sensitive to the call of the multitudes from other directions from that day on. They even sought out places where Bible study could be made available to unreached masses. At one time the church was sponsoring seven mission projects.

3. That They May Have Life

There are more than 48,000,000 unreached people within the Southern Baptist Convention territory. Almost all of our present church buildings are filled to capacity, even though we have been witnessing the greatest building program that Southern Baptists, or any other denomination, have ever launched.

We must go into regions beyond, and go now. If we fail to warn the multitudes, they will die in their sins and their blood will be on our hands. Oh, Southern Baptists, multitudes lie in darkness and despair. Will we, at this late hour, rise up and meet this emergency and go into these unchurched areas and provide Bible study and a church program for those who need Christ?

Reports reveal that new Sunday schools grow at a much faster rate than do older ones. The first year of a new Sunday school the average is 65 to 100 net gain, while the average of all the Sunday schools last year was ten. Twenty-five thousand new stations—branch Sunday schools, missions, or churches—could not begin to accommodate the spiritual needs of those who wait in darkness.

Providing for and reaching these people for Christ is not optional with Christians. It is the divine command, "Ye are witnesses of these things" (Luke 24:48). The best-known way we have to reach these people and reach them fast is to go where they are and make Bible study so convenient for them that they cannot reject it. This can be done by starting enough new Sunday schools.

Many of these unreached people will not come to our present churches. In one community less than four city blocks from the First Baptist Church, there lived sixty people who had never been in Sunday school. Some of them even remarked, "First Baptist Church will never come down here with a mission." They thought that no one was concerned about them, but when a Sunday school was started just for them in their little community, they responded beautifully. Now they act differently. They look different. In fact, they are different. That story could and should be duplicated hundreds of times in our Convention territory.

4. That God May Be Glorified

Starting new Sunday schools is at the heart of the work of evangelism. This type of work honors God; it magnifies Christ; it manifests the Bible. It reaches the lost for Christ. It disturbs the devil. It causes rejoicing in heaven. It brings glory and honor to God.

5. A Blessing to the Mother Church

New Sunday schools do something for the mother church. Sponsored work proves a blessing to those sponsoring it. New Sunday schools will put new life, a new spirit, and a new joy into the hearts of the people who have part in them. They give a sense of satisfaction that God's will is being done. Sponsoring work creates in a church the spirit that "everybody is somebody," because so many people are used who have never been used before.

One pastor writes: "The blessings and benefits came in an entirely different manner to what we thought when we moved into regions beyond. We thought it would just be a blessing to the unreached people, but it proved rather to bless our entire church. The pastor, the deacons, the membership all have been blessed."

Another pastor exclaimed: "What a blessing! When we started our first branch Sunday school, we had 1,100 members. Now we have started three Sunday schools. All three have become churches with a total membership of 1,875. Our church has grown to a membership of 2,445. What a blessing it is to sponsor new work!"

In what other way could a pastor lead his church to reach 4,320 people in a matter of three or four years?

II. MORE NEW TESTAMENT CHURCHES ARE NEEDED

There is serious thought today among Southern Baptist leaders that we can and should start at least 25,000 new churches and mission stations within the next few years.

1. Places Are Available

Are there unchurched areas in which to start churches? Are there potential workers to maintain them? Are there unreached multitudes that need them? There are 30,000 available places, more perhaps, where we ought to start new Sunday schools. There are three thousand cities in the territory of Southern Baptists with a population of twenty-five thousand to more than a million. Only a very few of these cities have more than one-half enough Baptist churches. What about your city? Is there a church within practical reach of every person?

Until Bible study is made available within easy reach of every member of every family, there are not enough churches in a community. Just how far people will go to church depends on their attitudes. Interested, enlisted people will cross a city to get to a church, but the ones who need reaching are not interested. They must have their interest quickened. The average church will not interest many who are not within easy reach. Some suggest that there should be a church within seven city blocks of every person.

There is need for more churches in the big cities and in the smaller ones. There are literally hundreds of new communities that have built up in recent years where there is not a genuine voice for Christ. People in the open country must be reached. There are possibilities for new churches and mission stations in thousands of places.

2. *Unreached Multitudes Are Available*

More than 48,500,000 people, not enlisted anywhere in Sunday school, live within the territory where Southern Baptists work. More than 21,000,000 of these people are out beyond the practical reach of a Southern Baptist church. They are so near, yet so far.

The Bible gives us a very vivid picture of Jesus weeping over a city in which perhaps 25,000 people lived. There are 3,000 cities in the territory where Southern Baptists work each of which has as many or more people than Jerusalem had. Some of these cities are totally unchurched. Bible study as you know it is not available for the people. What a glorious opportunity! Every existing church could and should respond to this call. There are literally thousands of places, with arms outstretched from the masses, where Sunday schools and churches should be started.

3. *Every Church Can and Should Mother Another*

Churches should be started and sponsored by existing churches. It proves a blessing to both the sponsoring church and the one sponsored. When this happens, a new day will dawn for the kingdom of God. Churches are great kingdom builders. Too often they get started the wrong way.

4. *Baptists Are Well Able*

Baptist churches have the money necessary to start 25,000 additional churches. They have in their possession enough of God's money to maintain them. They have the potential workers, yet idle, many of whom could say, "No man hath hired me, Lord." All too many people have never been asked to work.

Baptist churches have the message—the one message from a righteous God to an unrighteous people—the message of reconciliation. This message reveals God in Christ reconciling the world unto himself. With the message, the money, the workers, the commission from Christ, and the promise of the power and presence of the Holy Spirit, what else is necessary?

5. *Southern Baptists Know How*

Baptist churches know how to reach people. They have learned that new units grow faster and that the more units maintained, the more people reached. Southern Baptists know how to start and maintain churches. This makes the responsibility even greater. "Therefore to him that knoweth to do good, and doeth it not, to him it is sin" (James 4:17). Let no one come short in this vital matter!

6. *Southern Baptist Churches Have Been Blessed*

God continues his blessings upon Southern Baptist churches. He would bless many others if we had them. There is need for many more. Will you get your church to start one? It will prove a blessing to your church to be the mother of another. In fact, people who have started and sponsored new work testify that the greatest blessing comes to the mother church.

III. New Churches Are Invaluable to a Community

A New Testament church in a community makes a world of difference.

1. *New Churches Enlist Unenlisted Baptists*

There are more than 2,000,000 "lost, strayed, or stolen" members of Southern Baptist churches who need to be located and enlisted in the service of a church.

2. *Churches Are the Preserving Element of a Community*

When a New Testament church is organized in a community, it makes a difference. Like salt, it serves to preserve and keep a community from rot and decay. It makes all the difference in a community when there is a New Testament church in it.

3. *Churches Build Christian Homes*

The slogan of the Cradle Roll department of Southern Baptist Sunday schools is "A Christian Home for Every Baby." The quickest, easiest, and only way to a Christian home for a baby is to win its parents to Christ. Christian parents produce Christian homes.

4. *Churches Offer Opportunities to Preach the Gospel*

"It pleased God by the foolishness of preaching to save them that believe" (1 Cor. 1:21). People must hear the Word. "How shall they hear without a preacher? And how shall they preach, except they be sent?" (Rom. 10:14–15). The answer is New Testament churches.

5. *Churches Find and Develop the Best That Is in People*

There are other good agencies, institutions, and organizations in our cities and communities; but none other can do for people what a New Testament church does.

A church is the place where most people receive Christ

as Lord and Saviour. The warm spiritual atmosphere of a church service brings men to submit to the convicting power of the Holy Spirit. Nothing can take the place of public worship. Most people who follow Christ do so through the influence of a church service. Isaiah was in the Temple when he had the vision of the Lord that caused him to make his decision. After he saw the Lord, he saw himself and also a lost world. Then he said, "Here am I; send me" (Isa. 6:8).

A growing church offers a place for Christian fellowship. It offers its members a place of service which results in their development in the Christian graces. A growing church offers the individual an opportunity for going into all the world and preaching the gospel to every creature. My Co-operative Program dollar, given through my church, builds hospitals in Africa, Japan, and the Isles of the Sea. It preaches the gospel everywhere we have missionaries. It makes it possible for me to be a missionary every day, everywhere Southern Baptists do work.

A growing New Testament church offers opportunities for laying up treasures in heaven. It is "God's storehouse" for its members. The whole tithe is God's, and every Christian should bring it regularly into the storehouse "that there may be meat in mine house" (Mal. 3:10).

6. *Churches Help God Call Out the Called*

All too many times men have failed to respond to the call of God because the fires of evangelism burned low in their church. A growing, thriving New Testament church will prepare hearts to make the decision to follow Christ. In one church, during a period of two years of active promotion of branch Sunday schools, ten men surrendered to preach the gospel and three others to full-time education and music. The fires of evangelism were burning brightly.

7. *Churches Maintain Other Christian Institutions*

Churches are the only means of genuine missions and evangelism.

If it were not for Christian churches, there would be no Christian schools. Therefore build and grow more churches and so undergird and strengthen more Christian schools and other Christian institutions for the betterment of society and for the glory of God.

IV. How to Start New Work

"Everybody's business is nobody's business" all will agree. Therefore someone must be elected to be definitely in charge of this responsibility.

1. *Have an Associational Superintendent of Enlargement and Evangelism*

Every association, if properly organized, has a superintendent of enlargement and evangelism. This associational officer is charged with the responsibility to work with the corresponding officers in every church in the association in a program to church properly every area.

2. *Establish a Department of New Work in Each Church*

Each church in the association should set up a department of missions or new work and elect a superintendent of enlargement and evangelism to head the department. This officer will work with the corresponding officer of the association. Without these two key people it is hard to make much progress in starting new work.

3. *Secure Executive Committee Approval*

It is advisable to work along with the executive committee of the association in determining places where new work should start. Some few people still have the idea that there are too many churches. Fewer people, however, think that today than twenty years ago.

4. *Select Locations*

Make a survey of the needs in order to determine the locations for new work. Each church may be called upon to make a survey of its surrounding territories. Or the association may organize the various churches and make a city-wide or association-wide survey. Be sure to locate properly each branch Sunday school.

5. *Enlist Sponsoring Churches*

Each new Sunday school ought to have a sponsor. Each new church ought to have a mother. The associational superintendent of enlargement and enlistment should, under the direction of the executive committee, help to enlist a sponsoring church for each new work that is to be started. The nearest church to the area in which new work is to be started should be enlisted to sponsor the work, if at all possible. However, after the approach has been made, should the nearest church not feel that it is practical for them to extend their arms in that direction, the committee must contact another church.

6. *Secure the Workers*

Enlist the workers for each new Sunday school.

(1) *Elect a superintendent for each branch school.*—This, of course, is the duty of each church sponsoring a Sunday school. The one elected to be superintendent of the new work should be one of the warm hearts of the church, one who is really sold on the idea of moving out into unchurched areas and providing Bible study for the people who are unreached. Jesus said, "Pray ye therefore the Lord of the harvest, that he will send forth labourers into his harvest." God has people ready to do this. Our duty is to seek them out after much prayer.

(2) *Enlist and elect the officers and teachers.*—There are millions of undiscovered teachers and officers on the rolls of Southern Baptist churches who could be enlisted, either in the churches or in branch Sunday schools. There is unlimited man power lying in waste in every church. Many people have never been enlisted for service. They have not been trained, but if given an opportunity, they will do their best to qualify.

(3) *Call an associate pastor for the mission if possible.*
—Many have found it practical, in most cases, to organize a
full program like that in the mother church as soon as the
new Sunday school is started. If so, an associate pastor may
be called by the sponsoring church to assist in the new work
and to be responsible, in the main, for the work of the mission. It should be clearly understood that the mission pastor
is employed by the sponsoring church and not by the mission itself.

There must be a complete understanding and a close fellowship between the pastor of the sponsoring church, the
mission committee, and the mission pastor. He must be co-
operative in spirit and in service in all of his relationships
with the mother church.

7. Select a Meeting Place

Secure a meeting place for each branch Sunday school.
Some of our churches had their early beginnings in a living
room, a garage, or a shop of some kind. Start a branch Sunday school under a tree, on a boat, in a barbershop. Rent,
buy, or build a house, and someday a New Testament church
will be constituted.

8. Adopt Policies

Plans and policies for a branch Sunday school should be
adopted by the sponsoring church. The workers who go to
the mission must thoroughly understand that they are under
the sponsorship of the mother church. Of course, the members of the mission Sunday school will be a part of the
school of the sponsoring church. Those who come to unite
with the church through the mission arm will become members of the sponsoring church. Separate rolls should be kept
so that it will be easy to know exactly the names of those
who constitute the mission.

All tithes and offerings of new work sponsored should be
put into the general church treasury. All the bills of the
sponsored work should be paid by the treasurer of the spon-

soring church, in keeping with the financial policy of that church. The sponsoring church should underwrite all essential needs of the new work. It should be understood that the initial cost of the buildings and grounds will be taken care of by the sponsoring church.

The policy on purchasing must be understood by all. No purchase should be made by anyone for the church, or work sponsored, without a properly signed purchase order. Monthly reports should be made, both to the church and to the new work, of all the money received and disbursed. When plans and policies are adopted by the church and carried out in the right spirit, there will be a happy relationship between the sponsor and the work sponsored.

V. WHEN SHOULD A MISSION BECOME A CHURCH?

There are many cases where a branch Sunday school or mission has been constituted into a church before it was ready. On the other hand, some churches have delayed in leading their missions to become churches to the hurt of the work. A new work should become a church as soon as possible after it is strong enough, because many people who would hesitate to line up with a mission will come into a constituted church. There is, however, such a thing as too much haste in constituting a church. The two major things of importance in organizing a new church seem to be finances and leadership.

1. *Financial Strength*

It has never seemed wise to encourage a group to become a church until they are financially able to carry on the work to the good of the cause. A financial program would, of course, include pastor's salary, sufficient money for all local needs, and a reasonable amount to support the work around the world. When it is known that the financial income of a mission is insufficient to carry on the work, then it seems unwise to constitute it into a church. It is far easier to secure the assistance of the sponsoring church while a work remains a mission than after it becomes a church. Any sponsoring church should always be willing and ready to organize a mission into a church when it becomes strong enough to assume its financial obligations and provide its own leaders. Sponsoring churches should rejoice over such achievements.

2. *Adequate Leadership*

Experience has shown that most of the workers who start branch Sunday schools or work in mission points must be provided by the sponsoring church. Therefore it never seems wise to constitute a church until the local group can provide adequate leadership to carry on the work in an adequate and efficient manner. It takes time to enlist and train leaders. No mission should be encouraged to become a church until it is sufficiently able to provide its own leadership.

VI. EXTEND ARMS TO THE PEOPLE NOW!

The day Southern Baptists catch the vision and respond to the call of the Christ of the multitudes, they will endeavor to go into every unchurched community with the gospel. Branch Sunday schools and churches will be started. Millions who are without Christ will come to see and accept him as their Lord and Saviour.

The chief of police in a certain city came in and sat down with his pastor and said, "Pastor, the mission program of our church has done more to clean up our city and relieve our city of juvenile and adult delinquency than all my police force could ever do." That church had seven arms extended out to the people. Christian friends, we have the answer. Christ is the answer.

Is there a Sunday school or church within practical reach of every member of every family in your association? If not, why not start one now? There are some who will not come to your church. They may live next door; they may live in the next block; or they may live outside the city. Various are the reasons why they will not come. Someone should see to it that they have an opportunity to go to a church that would meet their needs.

A larger percentage of people are reached for Bible study, for Christ, for salvation, and for service in communities where churches are within easy reach. This explains why people of all denominations will go to and rally around a community church for at least a while. It is within easy reach. It is in their community. The way to reach people, reach them fast, and reach more of them is to see that every community is well churched. A Baptist church within easy reach of every member of every family should be the goal of Southern Baptists. This would be pleasing to God. Will Southern Baptists rise up, accept this task, move out into unpossessed territory, and claim it for God? Time will tell.

QUESTIONS FOR REVIEW

1. Why churches and Sunday schools any way?
2. Do we need fewer or more churches today?
3. Who is responsible for starting new work?
4. How can my church start and sponsor new work?

DIRECTIONS FOR THE TEACHING AND STUDY
OF THIS BOOK FOR CREDIT

I. DIRECTIONS FOR THE TEACHER

1. Ten class periods of forty-five minutes each, or the equivalent, are required for the completion of a book for credit.

2. The teacher should request an award on the book taught.

3. The teacher shall give a written examination covering the subject matter in the textbook. The examination may take the form of assigned work to be done between the class sessions, in the class sessions, or as a final examination.

EXCEPTION: All who attend all of the class sessions; who read the book through by the close of the course; and who, in the judgment of the teacher, do the classwork satisfactorily may be exempted from taking the examination.

4. Application for Sunday school awards should be sent to the state Sunday school department on proper application forms. These forms should be made in triplicate. Keep the last copy for the church file, and send the other two copies.

II. DIRECTIONS FOR THE STUDENT*

1. *In Classwork*

(1) The student must attend at least six of the ten forty-five minute class periods to be entitled to take the class examination.

(2) The student must certify that the textbook has been read. (In rare cases where students may find it impracticable to read the book before the completion of the classwork, the teacher may accept a promise to read the book

---

* The student must be fifteen years of age or older to receive Sunday school credit.

carefully within the next two weeks. This applies only to students who do the written work.)

(3) The student must take a written examination, making a minimum grade of 70 per cent, or qualify according to *Exception* noted above.

2. *In Individual Study by Correspondence*

Those who for any reason wish to study the book without the guidance of a teacher will use one of the following methods:

(1) Write answers to the questions printed in the book, or

(2) Write a development of the chapter outlines.

In either case the student must read the book through.

Students may find profit in studying the text together, but where awards are requested, individual papers are required. Carbon copies or duplicates in any form cannot be accepted.

All written work done by such students on books for Sunday school credit should be sent to the state Sunday school secretary.

III. This Book Gives Credit in Section IV of the Sunday School Training Course.

Date Due